Martyrdom: A Very Short Introduction

VERY SHORT INTRODUCTIONS are for anyone wanting a stimulating and accessible way in to a new subject. They are written by experts, and have been published in more than 25 languages worldwide.

The series began in 1995, and now represents a wide variety of topics in history, philosophy, religion, science, and the humanities. The VSI library now contains more than 300 volumes—a Very Short Introduction to everything from ancient Egypt and Indian philosophy to conceptual art and cosmology—and will continue to grow in a variety of disciplines.

Very Short Introductions available now:

Available soon:

For more information visit our website
www.oup.com/vsi/

Jolyon Mitchell

# MARTYRDOM

A Very Short Introduction

OXFORD
UNIVERSITY PRESS

# OXFORD
UNIVERSITY PRESS

Great Clarendon Street, Oxford, OX2 6DP,
United Kingdom

Oxford University Press is a department of the University of Oxford.
It furthers the University's objective of excellence in research, scholarship,
and education by publishing worldwide. Oxford is a registered trade mark of
Oxford University Press in the UK and in certain other countries

© Jolyon Mitchell 2012

The moral rights of the author have been asserted

First Edition published in 2012

Impression: 1

British Library Cataloguing in Publication Data
Data available

Library of Congress Cataloging in Publication Data
Data available

ISBN 978-0-19-958523-6

Printed in Great Britain by
Ashford Colour Press Ltd, Gosport, Hampshire

# Contents

# Acknowledgements

Thanks to Andrea Keegan, Emma Marchant, and Deborah
Protheroe at Oxford University Press for all their help with this *Very
Short Introduction*. I am also very grateful to the anonymous
reviewers for their careful reading and constructive suggestions, as
I am to Jacqueline Harvey, Theodora Hawksley, Clare Mitchell, and
David Smith for giving up so much time to read over various drafts. I
am indebted to staff at New College Library and the main
Edinburgh University Library, the National Library of Scotland, the
University Library in Cambridge, the Bodleian Library in Oxford,
the Rizal Library in Manila, the University of Tehran, and both the
Christian and State University in St Petersburg. It has been
invaluable to see, to touch, and to read a wide range of original texts,
images, and secondary sources in the flesh. I have learnt much not
only by discussing and lecturing on the topic of martyrdom, but also
by listening to scholars in Edinburgh and beyond.

I have found the observations and generosity of colleagues, friends,
teachers, and students extremely helpful. Thanks to Nick Adams,
Becky Artinian-Kaiser, Michael Banner, David Bebbington,
Stewart Brown, Peter Chelkowski, George Conyne, Jane Dawson,
Eamon Duffy, Alison and Jo Elliot, David Fergusson, Paul Foster,
Gene Garthwaite, Hugh Goddard, Christiane Gruber, Susan
Hardman-Moore, Paul Hobbs, Hannah Holtschneider, Stewart
Hoover, Larry Hurtado, David Jasper, Tim Jenkins, Tim Jones,

Elizabeth Koepping, Christian Lange, Gordon Lynch, Diarmaid MacCulloch, David Maxwell, Birgit Meyer, Paul Middleton, David Morgan, George Newlands, Michael Northcott, Joan Lochwood O'Donovan, Oliver O'Donovan, Nacim Pak-Shiraz, Paul and Sara Parvis, Stephen Pattison, Jamie Pitts, Kevin Reinhart, Scott Ross, Anne Sa'adah, Vit Sisler, Geoffrey Stevenson, Roxanne Varzi, George Wilkes, David Wright, Jenny Wright, and many others for their wise suggestions, insightful comments, and encouragement. Brief sections in Chapters 4 and 6 have been updated and adapted from earlier publications by the author, which are cited in the Further reading section at the end of the book, with thanks to Routledge. The research discussions and presentations on martyrdom and terrorism initiated by Dominic Janes, and including Asma Afsaruddin, David Andress, Akil N. Awan, Guy Beiner, Kate Cooper, Julia Douthwaite, Alex Houen, James Korke-Webster, Gabriel Koureas, Greg P. Kucich, Susannah Monta, Ronald Schechter, and Gary Waller were invaluable.

Thanks to Iona Birchall, John and Sarah Birchall, Janet and Kit Bowen, Katharine and Matthew Frost, Anna King, F. Ellis Leigh, Alexander and Nadine Matheson, Sorour and Hamish Matheson, Fiona and Richard Parsons, and my father Peter Mitchell and my mother Catharine Beck, who in different ways have helped make writing this book possible. Once again a huge thank you to Clare, who has engaged and journeyed with many of the pages that follow. Finally, thanks to our children Sebastian, Jasmine, and Xanthe, whose sense of humour and delight in life remain an inspiration.

# List of illustrations

Martyrdom

# Chapter 1
# Debating martyrdom

What precisely is martyrdom, and who can be called a martyr? In many corners of the world statues, shrines, and murals preserve memories of martyrs and martyrdom. Martyrs are also commemorated through films, posters, and websites. These physical and digital memorials inspire both devotion and debate. According to one version of the *Oxford English Dictionary*, a martyr is 'a person who is killed because of their religious or other beliefs', and martyrdom is 'the sufferings and death of a martyr'. In its various forms of common usage, martyrdom is a slippery term that is hard to define. This is partly because, as we shall see through this *Very Short Introduction*, there are many different kinds of martyrdom, emerging out of a range of historical, political, and religious settings.

For those unfamiliar with earlier historical contexts, martyrdom is increasingly known through descriptions found within contemporary news media. In many reports martyrdom is now commonly connected with a death that also results in the killing of others. Some scholars describe this as 'predatory martyrdom'. While predatory martyrdom is by no means the only kind of martyrdom that will be considered in this book, following the fatal attacks of 11 September 2001 in Manhattan, 11 March 2004 in Madrid, and 7 July 2005 in London, as well as recurring incidents in Afghanistan, Iraq, and other parts of the Middle East, there has been an increased interest in what drives some people to give up their lives in an attempt to kill many others. Obviously this is a highly contested practice.

One community's 'martyr' is another's 'terrorist'; one person's 'martyrdom operation' is another's 'suicide bombing'. The suicide bomber who makes a 'martyrdom video' before they blow themselves up, intent on also killing as many others as possible, believes that they will become a martyr. Others consider that these actions represent 'false' or 'pseudo' martyrdoms, which should not be classed alongside other forms of martyrdom, where the martyr embraces death in a non-violent fashion. For this reason many commentators claim that such attacks should not be described as martyrdom but rather as murder. From this perspective, describing a 'suicide attack' as a martyrdom is a corruption of an original more peaceful ideal. In the shadows of such attacks some now refer to a 'cult of suicide bombing', while others see it as a form of 'asymmetrical warfare' employed by oppressed peoples against more powerful occupying forces.

Suicide attacks have sharpened current debates about the meaning and the place of martyrdom in the contemporary world. These debates revolve around distinguishing between predatory and peaceful martyrdoms, military and non-violent martyrdoms, or active and passive martyrdoms. Alongside debates related to defining martyrdom, there are also discussions connected with the description, categorization, and creation of martyrdom: Why are some deaths described as martyrdoms? What are the different kinds of martyrdom? Who creates a martyrdom? How are martyrs made? These can lead to further questions relating to the motivation of martyrs. Why are some people drawn towards giving up their lives as martyrs? What place does religion play in creating and inciting martyrs? These discussions can provoke questions about memory: Why are some martyrs and martyrdoms remembered more than others? In order to answer these questions and to understand the contemporary debates about martyrdom it is helpful to examine its diverse roots and expressions within different traditions.

Scholars of martyrdom have attempted to answer these questions in various ways. Four approaches stand out. First, there are writers who highlight the *creative* role of the individuals and communities that are left behind. They create martyrs and martyrdoms after the victim's death. From this perspective, martyrs are made to serve the religious, social, or political needs of the surviving community. These memories of martyrdoms are repeated, preserved, and expressed through a range of media. Secondly, there are researchers who underline the *evolutionary* nature of martyrdom. These scholars observe, for example, how in Jewish, Islamic, and Christian traditions the meaning of the term 'martyrdom' has evolved. They also demonstrate that, as martyrdom stories are reiterated and translated, they are also adapted and elaborated upon. These observations sometimes lead to a third approach, which can be described as *evaluative*. Various commentators assert that in some cases there has been corruption of the original idea of martyrdom. From this view the ideal of martyrdom has been distorted or even hijacked by those who wish to wrest it violently into a way of asserting a particular world-view. Fourthly, there is an *inclusive* approach, which highlights the diverse nature of martyrdom. Scholars who take this approach largely eschew an evaluative approach, emphasizing instead the multifaceted and fragmentary nature of the phenomenon. This sometimes leads to a description of all possible forms of martyrdom in the most extended sense of the word, without necessarily investigating how individual traditions develop their own forms of criticism.

My aim in this *Very Short Introduction* is not only to explore these diverse approaches, but also to investigate how martyrdoms are portrayed (Chapter 2), remembered (Chapter 3), contested (Chapter 4), reformed (Chapter 5), politicized (Chapter 6), and questioned (Chapter 7). Both well-known and less well-known examples are used to explore how martyrdoms are created, used, and criticized. It is not my intention to offer a single theology or philosophy of martyrdom, nor to develop a substantive sociological thesis explaining the power of martyrdom. My aim is rather to draw on a wide range of examples to raise questions about martyrdom and to illuminate the different origins, kinds, and uses of martyrdom. My approach is more historically than theoretically driven, though the questions raised relate to a wide range of theories and academic disciplines. Many of the stories considered in this book are of individuals or groups who refused to compromise or to 'settle for half' and instead gave up their lives. They sacrificed themselves for many different reasons. These deaths are like question marks, interrogating the action of the victim, of the perpetrator, and of the spectator.

News about different kinds of martyrdom can spread rapidly, and to a wide range of audiences. It is now possible for stories of both contemporary and ancient martyrs to be transmitted instantaneously around the globe. Even the most sophisticated communication systems in the ancient world created by the Persian and Roman empires were effectively limited by the speed of the horse's hooves or ship's sails. Without printing, broadcasting, and, more recently, digital technologies, news about martyrdom took many weeks, months, and years to spread beyond its original setting. Nonetheless, in the pre-electronic era some spaces became inextricably connected with past martyrdoms, where streets, squares, and buildings are named after martyrs. This was one way, among many, that stories about martyrdom were preserved, remembered, and elaborated upon. This practice has continued into the digital age, with countless websites acting as virtual memorials of individuals who are described as having 'given up their lives' for their beliefs, their communities, or their nations. News about martyrdom is now more widely disseminated than ever before. This both encourages some individuals to seek maximum publicity as they give up their lives, and extends the debates relating to martyrdom.

Whatever one's personal attitude towards martyrdom, there is something unsettling about imagining ourselves into the world of an individual who embraces death and sacrifices their life. There is wisdom in treading carefully over these memories, as some died in considerable agony and some caused heartbreak through their deaths. Such attentiveness to different kinds of martyrdom will not inhibit critical questioning of the stories that follow. In his short story *The Portrait of Mr W. H.* (1889), Irish writer Oscar Wilde (1854–1900) has one of the characters declare that 'A thing is not necessarily true because a man dies for it'. Martyrdom may be evidence of intense belief, but it does not prove the accuracy of those beliefs. Not everyone who is described as a martyr dies for passionate beliefs, nor do they choose death. While some individuals almost stumble into becoming martyrs by accident, other people desire, embrace, and even seek martyrdom.

# Chapter 2
# Portraying martyrdom

There are currently lively discussions relating to the origins, evolution, and contemporary representations of martyrdom. A number of stories occur again and again in both popular and scholarly accounts of martyrdom. They are used across various religious traditions and academic disciplines. Just as well-known paintings have been examined from many different angles, these portrayals of martyrdom have been scrutinized close up and at a distance. They have often travelled many miles and been viewed by many pairs of eyes. They have been talked over, written about, and copied. Like pictures in an art gallery, some attract curious crowds, while others are left to the specialists or even entirely overlooked.

Styles, fashions, and taste change. So too does the way in which martyrdoms are depicted by painters, film-makers, and other storytellers. It is possible to encounter realistic, romantic, and impressionistic portrayals of martyrdom. These depictions are used to illustrate arguments, inspire devotion, and bring history to life. They are repeated, added to, and elaborated upon. They are put to use in different ways in distinct historical contexts. Some are even viewed as 'founding martyrdoms', though each portrayal has its own complex biography, many stretching back hundreds of years. Several stories of martyrdom particularly stand out.

While the following examples are widely cited and are sometimes viewed as 'original' martyrs, they also illuminate two closely related types of martyrdom, the 'noble death' tradition and the 'voluntary violent death' tradition. These are not static traditions set in stone; rather, they are constantly evolving.

## The noble death

One of the best-known paintings in New York's Metropolitan Museum of Art is Jacques-Louis David's *Death of Socrates* (1787) (Figure 1). Set in what looks like a prison cell against the backdrop of a grey stonewall is a bearded man, wearing a light toga, perched upright on a wooden bed; one hand points upwards, while the other reaches for a wide-rimmed bronze-coloured goblet. He is placed at the focal point of the picture, in the centre. The cup is held by a younger man who turns away, covering his eyes with his fingers. Most viewers in the 18th century would have known what the cup contains: hemlock. Socrates' commanding figure, his chest exposed, his face calm,

1. Jacques-Louis David, *The Death of Socrates*, oil on canvas, 1787

stands in sharp contrast to the men who surround him: some weep, cover their faces, or are transfixed in grief. His family are led away up the stairs. Apart from the stoical figure of Socrates, only two seated figures, probably Plato at the head of the bed and Crito, retain any sense of emotional control. David's painting commends the virtue of facing death stoically. Here is a philosopher standing firm in the midst of anguish. Painted on the eve of the French Revolution, this painting not only reflects contemporary 18th-century concerns, but also invites viewers to go back over 2,000 years to Socrates' death in 399 BCE.

While the artist David (1748–1825), initially an energetic supporter of the French Revolution, drew on a number of sources for inspiration for his oil painting, some viewers would have known the story behind this picture from Plato's accounts in his *Apology* and the *Phaedo*. In the *Apology*, through the form of a dialogue Plato (c.424–348 BCE) describes Socrates' (c.469–399 BCE) trial, where he mounts his own defence and takes on his accusers: 'I would rather die having spoken in my manner, than speak in your manner and live.' He questions the wisdom of doing 'anything' to escape death. 'For often in battle there is no doubt that if a man will throw away his arms, and fall on his knees before his pursuers, he may escape death, if a man is willing to say or do anything.' For Socrates, as described by Plato, 'the difficulty . . . is not in avoiding death, but in avoiding unrighteousness; for that runs deeper than death'. There is a powerful simplicity in Socrates' reported words: 'The hour of departure has arrived, and we go our ways, I to die and you to live. Which is the better, only God knows.'

Socrates was ordered to drink hemlock after the Athenian senate narrowly voted him guilty of 'denying the Gods and corrupting the young'. It appears that he may have rejected the opportunity to go into exile on the grounds that death would be a better form of escape. The eponymous narrator in Plato's *Phaedo* offers a description of Socrates' dignified death:

he raised the cup to his lips and very cheerfully and quietly drained it. Up to that time most of us had been able to restrain our tears fairly well, but when we watched him drinking and saw that he had drunk the poison, we could do so no longer, but in spite of myself my tears rolled down in floods, so that I wrapped my face in my cloak and wept for myself; for it was not for him that I wept, but for my own misfortune in being deprived of such a friend.

According to this account Socrates goes on to chide his friends for weeping, then stands up and walks around. Soon his legs go numb, as the poison takes its course and works its way up the rest of his body towards his heart. His last enigmatic words, a request of one of his friends to pay a small outstanding debt, have been interpreted as a subtle way of saying his death will plant a seed for freedom. Some later accounts would interpret his state-ordered suicide not only as a noble death, but also as a martyrdom. In other words, Socrates was seen as someone who was prepared to die for his beliefs. He has even been described as 'the first philosopher martyr', the 'first martyr for free speech', and the 'Western world's first recorded martyr'. While Plato and other ancient writers portrayed his death as a voluntary act, Plato appears to be using the dialogue, in which this story is embedded, to make an argument that even after death the soul survives.

The Athenian historian Xenophon (*c*.431–354 BCE) provides a different and probably slightly later perspective of the trial in his *Apology of Socrates to the Jury*, claiming that this was based upon the account of an eyewitness, Hermogenes, who like Plato appears to have been present at the trial. Xenophon describes how Socrates suggested that it would be better to die before the limitations of advanced ageing set in, such as the 'increasing dimness of sight', 'dullness of hearing', and loss of memory. Several recent interpreters have drawn upon both Plato and Xenophon's accounts to suggest that Socrates rejected a 'gentle death', and instead willingly embraced the role of 'scapegoat'. This has led some to argue that

Socrates intended his voluntary death not only to 'preserve philosophy' in Athens, but also to heal the rifts within Athenian society.

## Using noble deaths

How have these ancient accounts of Socrates' 'noble death' been re-presented in later contexts? Over 600 years later, several early church writers described Socrates as a pre-Christian martyr, though subsequent writers (such as John Chrysostom, c.347–407 CE) claimed that, compared to Socrates, the youthful Christian martyrs who were brutally put to death in the arena endured superior forms of martyrdom. Nonetheless, it is clear that other early Christian writers used Socrates' noble death to inform their understanding of martyrdom. This was a way of further validating Christian martyrdoms. The story of his trial and poisoning has continued to be cited, retold, and represented for over two millennia. For example, in his open 'Letter from a Birmingham Jail', Martin Luther King, Jr celebrates Socrates as one who 'practised civil disobedience' (16 April 1963). King appears less concerned with defining Socrates as a martyr than with using his story to support his own case for active non-violent resistance. Socrates' death has proved to be a useful resource from which to create new narratives.

As David's 18th-century painting illustrates, the stoical way in which Socrates embraced death has been long remembered and celebrated through different media. Over the last century his death has even attracted novelists, playwrights, and screenwriters. In John Steinbeck's novel, *The Moon is Down* (1942), the reader is invited into the world of a small mining town in northern Europe. Without identifying his subject explicitly as Norwegian resistance against the Germans during the Second World War, Steinbeck creates a story where locals become increasingly daring in their acts of resistance against the invading forces. The foreign occupiers take the mayor and his doctor friend hostage, threatening to kill them unless the local resistance ceases. In the final chapter, as he faces execution, the mayor recalls how at school he had recited part of Socrates' final speeches. In response to the question 'Are you not ashamed, Socrates, of a course of life which is likely to bring you to an untimely end?' he recalls how, playing Socrates, he had repeated the lines 'a man who is good for anything ought not to calculate the chance of living or dying; he ought only to consider whether he is doing right or wrong'.

En route to his death, echoing Socrates, the mayor encourages his friend to make sure that a debt is paid. In this coded way he tells his friend to ensure that the resistance continues even after his execution. In the film adaptation (1943), his wish is fulfilled as the movie ends with his death and a series of explosions caused by the local resistance fighters. *The Moon is Down* was also an extremely popular book during and after the Second World War. It was widely translated and secretly circulated and read all over occupied Europe. It was also adapted into a propagandistic play. By mirroring the story of Socrates' death Steinbeck was able to challenge the claim regularly made by the Axis powers that they were returning to a classical ideal, as well as reminding readers of Greece's recent predicament, for it too had been overrun by German and Italian forces in April 1941. Socrates' noble death was not only a martyrdom to be remembered: it was also a resource to be used in significantly different historical contexts. As these later literary, cinematic, and artistic adaptations of Socrates' dignified death illustrate, a dramatic historical martyrdom narrative not only reflects contemporary concerns, but can also provoke ethical or religious questions.

Some view Socrates' death as a suicide, others view it is a martyrdom, while for others the precise definition does not matter as it remains a dramatic story to be appropriated. Even those who question whether his death can be viewed as an actual martyrdom commonly portray his final moments as dignified, calm, and noble. This may partly explain why Socrates' death stands out even more than those in the ancient world who famously took their own lives to preserve their honour or to alleviate their shame, such as Anthony and Cleopatra when defeated (30 BCE),

Hannibal when cornered (182 BCE), and Lucretia when raped (*c.*508 BCE). While these are sometimes described as 'noble deaths', it is the final hours of the man sometimes described as the 'Father of Western Philosophy' that are more commonly used to exemplify the 'noble death' tradition and even the beginnings of martyrdom.

## Voluntary violent deaths

Not all martyrdoms appear to be as noble or dignified. Gustav Doré's (1832–83) *Martyrdom of Eleazer the Scribe* (Figure 2) is a more violent depiction than David's portrayal of the death of Socrates, with an aggressive gang of men clustering around a fallen elderly man. A knife pierces his abdomen, two spears are thrust at his body, and a whip is poised to strike. Bystanders observe passively. Created in the 19th century as one of many illustrations for an illustrated Bible (1866), this picture refers to and goes beyond the account of one of the earliest recorded martyrdoms, found in 2 Maccabees, and expanded in 4 Maccabees.

The stories of the so-called 'Maccabean Martyrs' from 2 Maccabees (6–7) are widely regarded as an important text for understanding various approaches to martyrdom. I am using them here primarily to reflect on the tradition of 'voluntary violent death'. The book of 2 Maccabees was written in Greek, mostly around 125–124 BCE, and probably emerged out of Alexandria, Egypt. It appears to have been intended for Greek-speaking Jews living outside their homeland. Like 1 Maccabees, it tells the story of the Maccabean Revolt, which eventually led in 142 BCE to the independence of the Jews from Seleucid rule. The Maccabean Revolt is commonly seen as a war of resistance against foreign rulers, priests who collaborated, and the imposition of alien customs. It is therefore possible to read 2 Maccabees simply as representing the conflict between faithful Judaism and defiling Hellenism. Some historians now argue that the situation was more complex, suggesting that the

2. Gustave Doré, *Martyrdom of Eleazer the Scribe*, woodcut, Doré's *English Bible*, 1866

Seleucid king Antiochus Epiphanes IV (215–164 BCE) intervened
in Judaea to quell internal Jewish conflicts between traditionalists,
who wished to preserve Jewish purity, and Hellenizers, who were
more open to Greek cultural influences. Whatever his motivations,
2 Maccabees portrays Antiochus attempting to outlaw Jewish
practices and customs, and the fierce resistance that this
provoked.

In 2 Maccabees 6 the reader is told how 'the king sent out an Athenian elder to force the Jews to turn away from their ancestral laws and stop living according to God's laws'. The temple was defiled, statues to the Olympian God Zeus were brought inside, and it was even used for sex with prostitutes. Two 'women who had circumcised their sons' were dragged around the city and then thrown from the city walls, while others were burnt for attempting to keep the Sabbath. These deaths, not always viewed as martyrdoms, provide a broader context for the stories that follow.

The narrator then steps in and encourages readers not to be depressed by such tales, underlining that such experiences are not for the 'destruction of our people but for their discipline' and that God will not forsake his people. He goes on to tell the story of Eleazer, a 'leading scribe', 'elderly in age and with a most dignified outward appearance', who is 'compelled' to eat pork which has been sacrificed to idols. The narrator then describes how he 'preferred death with honour' than 'life with religious defilement', and so spat out the meat. We then learn that those persecuting him had known him for a long time, and so took him to one side to suggest that he 'pretend' to eat the meat so as to 'escape death'. In response Eleazar adopted a 'dignified manner worthy of his seniority' and his 'distinguished old age and the grey hair he had acquired', declaring that:

> It is not worthy of our old age to act out such a role. Otherwise, many of the young would assume wrongly that Eleazar the 90-year-old had changed to a foreign way of life. If I acted out this charade for the sake of living a moment longer, I would mislead them, and I would be defiled and be dishonoured in my old age. Even if I escaped the punishment of human beings for the moment, I would certainly not escape the hands of the almighty—whether alive or dead. So I give up my life courageously now to show myself worthy of my old age, and to leave a fine example for the young people of how to die a good death with eagerness and dignity for the revered and sacred laws.

14

His listeners were then enraged and he was beaten to death. As he was about to die he groaned: 'It is clear to the Lord with his sacred knowledge that, although I could have been saved from death, I endure in my body harsh pain from this beating, yet in my soul I cheerfully suffer these things because I respect him.' The narrator claims this is 'a most noble and memorable example of virtue not only for the youth but also for the majority of his nation' (2 Maccabees 6:1–31).

His 'memorable' example is followed immediately in the next chapter, 2 Maccabees 7, by the gruesome story of a mother who sees her seven sons brutally tortured and then executed for refusing to eat pork. Each son makes a short affirmation of faith before he is executed, though they never mention Eleazar's 'noble' example. Several declare their belief in the resurrection and the punishment of their persecutors. The sixth son declares: 'We suffer these things because of our own sins against our God.' The mother is particularly commended by the narrator as 'the most remarkable of all', who 'deserves to be remembered with special honour' because 'she watched her seven sons die in the space of a single day', in an agonizing fashion, 'yet she bore it bravely because she put her trust in the Lord'. These martyrdom stories are used as examples of steadfastness and bravery in the face of persecution and extreme suffering, to admire, learn from, and perhaps emulate.

Unlike the stories in the Hebrew Bible of Shadrach, Meshach, and Abednego (their Hebraic names were Hananiah, Mishael, and Azariah) in the fiery furnace (Daniel 1–3) or of Daniel in the lion's den (Daniel 6), there is no supernatural deliverance for those who hold firmly to the law. The elderly Eleazer and the mother with her seven sons are all killed. These are rare examples of voluntary death in a book that celebrates forms of holy war against foreign oppressors. The narrative in 2 Maccabees 8 swiftly moves from these martyrdom tales to the success of Judas Maccabaeus in raising an army of 6,000 troops in secret, in his guerrilla warfare, and ultimately in his war against the Seleucid oppressors. How is this possible? The narrator provides a somewhat surprising and stark answer: Judas Maccabaeus 'could not be stopped' because 'the wrath of the Lord had turned to mercy' (2 Maccabees 8:5). Some interpreters suggest that the 'shed blood' of these martyrs cleansed the nation and placated God's anger against his people. Others reject this interpretation, though they do acknowledge that in the narrative of 2 Maccabees these martyrdoms mark a turning point in the fortunes of the Jewish people.

Their stories are retold in the later 4 Maccabees. In this book the author not only underlines the importance of devout reason over passion, but also makes clear the claim that Eleazar and the other martyrs' 'native land was purified through them' (4 Maccabees 1:11). The book of 4 Maccabees, written perhaps two centuries later than 1 and 2 Maccabees, expands on these earlier martyrdom stories while leaving out the resistance stories of Judas Maccabaeus and his fellow freedom fighters. The author of 4 Maccabees turns these martyrs into pivotal figures against the 'tyrant Antiochus' (5:1–7:23 and 8:1–18:24). In 4 Maccabees Eleazer is tortured more brutally, but endures like a 'noble athlete' and 'becomes young again through reason' in the face of suffering.

These Maccabean martyrdom stories have attracted considerable attention from scholars attempting to discern the roots of martyrdom. Their voluntary violent deaths are comparatively rare events. Some even regard Eleazar as the 'Father of Jewish Martyrdom', and the mother and the seven sons as his first 'faithful disciples'. Given such descriptions and the dramatic nature of their martyrdoms, it is surprising that these stories then largely disappeared from view for several decades. Jewish writers such as Philo (c.20 BCE–50 CE) and Josephus (c.37–100 CE) did not explicitly mention the Maccabean Martyrs, with Josephus paying more attention to the voluntary suicide, probably by killing each other, of some 900 men, women, and children at the fortress in Masada (73 CE). It is almost as though the narratives of Eleazar the scribe and of the mother and her seven sons were lost, repressed, or simply never retold.

Following the First Jewish–Roman War, which began in 66 CE, the subsequent fall of Jerusalem, and the destruction of the temple (70 CE), as well as the later unsuccessful Bar Kohba Revolt (132–5 CE), the priestly classes lost much of their original power. Judaism fragmented into a number of different rabbinic schools. Several rabbinic writers returned to these martyrdom stories, adapting them to fit their own situations. They relocated them in the time of the persecution under the Roman emperor Hadrian (76–138 CE): Eleazar the scribe vanished and the anonymous mother was given a name, Miriam, and took on a more significant and expressive role. In the new representation she is punished not for refusing pork, but rather for refusing to worship an idol. In other words, the original narratives were adapted and put to new uses in a fresh historical setting.

It was not until the 2nd century that the term *kiddush ha-Shem* (to die for the sanctification of the [Divine] Name), in Judaism, came to be understood as 'martyr'. It would soon be connected with the Maccabean Martyrs, who were later known as *Kedoshim*, because they had chosen death over the *hillul ha-Shem* (defamation of the [Divine] Name). In the midst of the persecutions by the emperor Hadrian, the rabbis held a secret council in Lydda, codifying laws relating to martyrdom: an individual was obliged to accept death rather than commit idolatry, unchastity (e.g., incest or adultery), and murder. Other commandments could be broken as long as fewer than ten Jews were present. This concern about public witness is reminiscent of Eleazar's expressed concern that he would set a bad example to the young. These rulings were not universally accepted and there was ambivalence towards the whole practice of martyrdom.

How to remember and to commemorate martyrdoms appears to have contributed to the separation of Judaism and Christianity, and their formation as distinct religious traditions with separate identities. Some scholars speak of a wave flowing between Judaism and Christianity as they began to separate, but these dramatic stories continued to flow between the related traditions for several hundreds of years.

## Using past martyrdoms

Within the Christian churches Eleazar, the mother and her seven sons came to be known as the 'Holy Maccabean Martyrs', and the sons as the 'Seven Maccabee Brothers', and were included on the calendar of saints' days by both the Roman Catholic and the Eastern Orthodox churches. Their stories were retold in a number of patristic (early Christian) sermons, as prefiguring later Christian martyrdoms. In several later Christian accounts they were given individual names, with the mother sometimes being called Solomonia. A number of medieval churches are named after the Maccabean Martyrs. In the church of St Andrew, Cologne, it is still possible to see a richly decorated golden shrine in their honour. Several medieval mystery plays brought their stories back to life. It is possible that the French Dance of Death or *Danse Macabre* originated from the Dance of the Maccabees, which re-enacted their martyrdoms. There are a wide range of Orthodox icons commemorating the Maccabean Martyrs. Again, their stories were put to very different uses than within Jewish communities.

This became more pronounced during the time of the Crusades in medieval Europe. After the start of the First Crusade in 1095, many of the crusaders did not wait until they reached the Holy Land to begin killing. The massacre of Ashkenazic Jews along the river Rhine (and Danube) during the spring and summer of 1096 inspired a new literature in response to the killings, with several accounts produced in the first half of the 12th century: *The Chronicle of Rabbi Eliezer bar Nathan*, *The Chronicle of Rabbi Solomon bar Simson*, and *The Narrative of the Old Persecutions*, which is sometimes known as *Mainz Anonymous*. How should

Jews respond when confronted by the choice to convert to Christianity or die? The authors drew upon earlier Jewish martyrological traditions such as the mother and her seven sons from Maccabees to emphasize continuity with the past, while also underlining the unique nature of these new persecutions. When some Jewish communities (such as at Mainz) chose to kill each other rather than suffering death at the hands of the crusaders, later writers would reference not the Maccabean Martyrs but the Masada 'heroes' or 'martyrs' who chose to die to save themselves from the swords of the Roman invaders.

Over the next three centuries both French and German Jewish writers retold stories about these and other Jewish martyrdoms, caused both by crusaders (1096, 1147, and 1188) and by locals who believed that Jewish communities were behind the murder of children in order to use the blood in their worship services, the desecration of the communion host, and even the Black Death (from 1348). For example, Ephraim ben Yaakov (1132–1200) describes how about forty Jews were killed at Blois following such accusations. They were given the choice of saving their lives if they left their religion and accepted Christianity. Yaakov describes how they refused even when 'beaten and tortured', encouraging 'each other to remain steadfast and die for the sanctification of God's Name'. Some writers went beyond narrative description to poetic lament, mourning these 'beautiful deaths' (*bele qedushah*).

Several of these poems resonate with earlier ancient stories. These narratives were resources to be used rather than constrictive tales to follow slavishly. These writers stood in an evolving tradition that interacted with earlier martyrdom accounts. Neither the Maccabees nor Socrates invented martyrdom. They were not the first ever martyrs. They are, however, illuminating examples of two different types of martyrdom stories. They have their distinctive origins in Greek and Jewish narratives. In the first, the noble death, both contemporaries and later generations celebrated how Socrates took his own life in a controlled and noble fashion. In the second, the voluntary violent death, the Maccabean Martyrs accepted and even welcomed their own brutal killing by another group. These are obviously not mutually exclusive categories, as Socrates remained in Athens and took his own life voluntarily, while some later writers also described the suicides at Masada and later Jewish martyrdoms as noble deaths. There are no clear criteria as to what makes for a 'noble death' or for a 'voluntary violent death'. The differences between these two traditions blur, especially because both have fictive, religious, and artistic lives beyond the original stories. These examples provide evidence of how martyrdom stories were used and evolved at the same time. These two closely related types, the noble death and the voluntary violent death, along with several other types, will be visible in many of the other examples in the pages that follow.

# Chapter 3
# **Remembering martyrdom**

In Jean-Léon Gérôme's painting *The Christian Martyrs' Last Prayer* (1883), more than thirty defenceless men, women, and children huddle together in the arena of the Colosseum, their hands clasped together in prayer (Figure 3). They studiously ignore the thousands of faceless spectators, the crucifixions, and the burning crosses that surround them. Their attention is not shaken by the appearance of a dark-golden lion on the sand. Death awaits these apparently passive but serene Christians. This artistic vision of martyrdom, depicted by an artist famous for his portrayals of the Middle East, is one example of many highly romanticized visions of martyrdom. It may be a romantic view, but it illustrates how the story of defenceless individuals embracing death for their faith holds an enduring fascination.

Even though this artistic vision emerged out of a 19th-century historical context, it nevertheless resonates with elements of the martyrdom literature from earliest Christian communities. These accounts had emerged from different contexts and at different times, commonly reflecting the distinct needs and interests of the writer or editor's own community. Some descriptions embellished the events, transforming the martyrs into early Christian saints with supernatural powers over the beasts, or the fires, or their gladiatorial executioners. This process of embellishment or elaboration has a long history, and continues

**3. Jean-Léon Gérôme, *The Christian Martyrs' Last Prayer*, oil on canvas, 1883**

up to the present time. While Gérôme (1824–1904) does not turn his central subjects into superheroes, there is a romantic quality to his vision that perhaps tells us more about his own 19th-century artistic tradition than the tradition of early Christian martyrdoms.

## The origins of martyrdom in early Christianity

What then did the word 'martyrdom' actually mean to the early Christians? The word 'martyr' derives from the Greek word *martus*, meaning 'witness', while the verb *martureo* is commonly translated 'to bear witness'. Initially these words were not inextricably connected with being a 'blood witness', in other words, bearing witness by giving up one's life to death. For example, the risen Christ predicts that his Apostles will be 'my witnesses in Jerusalem…and to the ends of the earth' (Acts 1:8). In the same chapter the apostle Peter uses the same word to speak of 'eyewitnesses to the resurrection' (Acts 1:22). With the intensification of persecution against early Christians the Greek term *martus* appears to have evolved from denoting a legal witness who provides testimony (e.g., John 1:15) or an eyewitness, to meaning those who endured hardships, and then to those who died for their Christian faith.

The precise dates of this linguistic evolution are debated, but there are signs that even within the earliest Christian documents both the noun ('witness') and the verb ('to bear witness') were beginning to be linked with bearing witness through suffering and death. Both words regularly recur in the New Testament, especially in John, Acts, and Revelation. Perhaps most significant is the way, in the book of Revelation, Jesus is described not only as the 'Christ' but also as 'the faithful witness' (Revelation 1:5). Even though this is rarely translated as 'faithful martyr', many scholars interpret this to mean that Jesus is viewed here as the 'proto-' or even 'founding martyr', who is then described as the 'firstborn from the dead'. From this point of view, Jesus is portrayed as both the pioneering martyr and the 'first' of many to overcome death. The idea that through his crucifixion Jesus was *the* exemplary martyr became common currency in the early church. Following a vivid description of the martyrdoms of several Christians in Gaul, the early church historian Eusebius of Caesarea (263–339 CE) commented that 'they were so eager to imitate Christ . . . they gladly yielded the title of martyr to Christ, the true Martyr and Firstborn from the dead' (*Ecclesiastical History* 5.2.3).

Revelation is commonly interpreted as a book addressed to early Christian communities facing persecution and martyrdom for their faith. The readers are encouraged 'not to be afraid of what you are about to suffer', or to give up if they are thrown into prison or when they are persecuted, and to remain faithful 'even unto death' (Revelation 2:10–11). The church community in Pergamum is affirmed for holding fast to their faith even when Antipas, a 'witness' (or 'martyr'), is killed. While Antipas is the only martyr named in the book, the theme recurs through Revelation. For example, there is a vast crowd of martyrs who have come out of the 'great tribulation', and are portrayed in white robes holding palm branches in their hands (7:9–17). Later in the book, during one of the apocalyptic visions, a female figure, 'Babylon the Great, the Mother of Prostitutes and Abominations of the Earth' (more popularly known as 'the Whore of Babylon'), is described as a 'woman drunk on the blood of the saints and of the blood of the martyrs of Jesus' (Revelation 17:6). One possible reason why Revelation was selected to be included within the authorized canon (collection) of books that made up the New Testament was because of its references to martyrs. As martyrdom stories became more popular here was a text, full of apocalyptic visions, which resonated with the experience of the early church, whose members both experienced and largely affirmed martyrdom. It is also probable that the book of Revelation influenced the development and content of subsequent martyr stories.

If Jesus is the proto-martyr who led the way through his own suffering and death, then it is Stephen who is often seen as the first martyr of the church. In the New Testament book, the Acts of the Apostles, Stephen delivers a speech which contains a provocative reading of Israel's history and which leads his enraged listeners to take him outside Jerusalem's walls and stone him to death, while Saul looks on (Acts 7:54–8:1). Stephen's last words are reminiscent of Jesus's words of forgiveness on the cross in the Gospel of Luke. The author of Acts (who also wrote Luke) regards the martyr Stephen as following in the footsteps of Jesus's death. Later in the same book Paul (who has changed his name from Saul after his conversion on the Damascus road) speaks to the religious leaders on a return visit to Jerusalem. There he describes Stephen as your 'witness', whose blood was shed, and how he himself had stood by and looked after the cloaks of those who had killed him (Acts 22:20). Stephen's story is commonly used as one of the foundational martyrdom narratives in later histories of the church. Several medieval and Renaissance artists also depicted his stoning (Figure 4). Towards the end of the 2nd century the word 'martyr' became more explicitly connected with the idea of a 'blood witness', someone who gave up their life for their faith. One of the earliest surviving accounts of a Christian martyrdom outside the

4. **Bernardo Daddi** (*c*.1280–*c*.1348), *Martyrdom of St Stephen* (detail, right side), fresco, *c*.1324 Daddi compresses Stephen's story from the book of Acts into a single fresco. On the left side (beyond this picture detail) listeners point, cover their ears and grab at his cloak. On this right side (above), he is being stoned. Three small rocks look as though they are already attached to his head and shoulder. At the same time, Stephen stares upwards and sees the 'heavens open and the son of the man standing at the right hand of God' (Acts 7:56)

New Testament, the *Martyrdom of Polycarp* (*c.*155), uses 'martyr' in this sense. It was probably not until middle of the 4th century that the term was used exclusively to mean someone who died for their Christian beliefs.

## Martyrdom and state persecution

Christians lived in a world where the violence at the heart of the state was sometimes directed against them. The first example of centrally orchestrated Roman persecution was by the emperor Nero in 64 CE. This scapegoating may have been carried out to distract attention from persistent rumours that he had started the great fire of Rome in July 64 to make more room for a new palace. The Roman historian Tacitus wrote concisely about the spectacular deaths:

> In their very deaths they were made the subjects of sport: for they were covered in the hides of wild beasts, and they expired from mutilation by dogs, or were burned fixed to crosses for use as nocturnal illumination on the dwindling of daylight. Nero offered his own garden players for the spectacle ... For this cause a feeling of compassion arose towards the sufferers, though guilty and deserving of exemplary capital punishment, because they seemed not to be cut off for the public good, but were victims of the ferocity of one man. (Tacitus, *Annals* 15.44)

There are debates about precisely how to translate this passage, and whether these early Christians were crucified, burnt, or set alight on crosses. If so, the punishment spoke graphically of the crime. If they had burnt Rome, then they 'deserved' to be burnt themselves. This dramatic form of execution, burning on a cross, has also been represented in other settings (e.g. Figure 3).

At first persecutions were sporadic and localized. It was well over 150 years before systematic empire-wide campaigns developed during parts of the reigns of emperors such as Decius (249–51),

Valerian (253–60), and Diocletian (284–305). These waves of persecution have been the subject of vigorous scholarly debates. Commentators have drawn on political, social, and theological insights to explain why some early Christians were killed. There has been a tendency to overestimate the total number of Christians who actually died as martyrs. The last 100 years have seen more sober estimates, with suggestions that it was probably only a tiny proportion of the early church that were actually martyred. There is growing recognition that the vast majority of ordinary Christians survived because of the sporadic nature of the persecutions, the laxness of some local officials, and the compromises they themselves made. Several historians claim that to survive some would comply, flee, dodge, lie, bribe their way to safety, hide in haylofts or cellars, but still identify themselves as Christians. These ordinary responses led to controversy over whether or how those who had lapsed were permitted to return to the fold. They also temper the illusion that most Christians were yearning for the opportunity to be martyred.

## Embracing martyrdom

Unlike the Roman Stoic philosopher Seneca who affirmed the courage of gladiators who killed themselves rather than face humiliation in the arena, Ignatius (*c.*35–*c.*107), the bishop of Antioch, wished to die as a public martyr in the amphitheatre. According to the church historian Eusebius, he did so in 108. Eusebius preserved a series of letters by Ignatius, who wrote these while being escorted by soldiers from Antioch to Rome and martyrdom. One theme that runs through several of Ignatius' letters is his seemingly irrational yearning to be wounded by his persecutors: 'For I do indeed desire to suffer, but I know not if I be worthy to do so' (*The Epistle of Ignatius to the Trallians* 4.1). Elsewhere he goes further. Even before the term 'martyr' had come exclusively to be connected with the idea of being a 'blood witness', Ignatius appears keen to be tortured and to be slain for his faith. This strain of what some would describe today as a

27

'masochistic tendency' is most explicit in his *Epistle to the Romans* where he makes several requests: not to be saved from martyrdom (2), for prayers that he will be martyred (3), and, more specifically, that he will be allowed to be fed to the wild beasts (4). Under the title of 'I desire to die' he states: 'Come, fire and cross, encounters with beasts, incisions and dissections, wrenching of bones, hacking of limbs, crushing of the whole body' (5.3). Unlike many modern martyrs, Ignatius desires violence to be done to his body, rather than to do violence to his enemies through his own death. One of his most famous metaphors illustrates not only his yearning for suffering, but also an implied hope that his death will result in a transformative good: 'I am the wheat of God and I am ground by the teeth of the beasts that I may be found pure bread' (5.1). It is as if he wants to become the broken bread to be eaten by his persecutors. Ignatius was not alone in seeking out execution for his faith. Choosing to follow in the footsteps of Christ to death and thereby hoping to make a final public statement in the amphitheatre became increasingly popular among zealous church groups in North Africa.

Voluntary or radical martyrdom, as it is sometimes described, soon became a subject of contention in the early church. Between the end of the 2nd century and the mid 3rd century a number of leading church figures argued against the practice of seeking out martyrdom, making a distinction between those who actively volunteered to die and those whose life was forfeited by the demands of the state. The bishop of Carthage, Cyprian (*c.*200–58), for example, made suggestions as to how the North African enthusiasm for martyrdom might be limited. In a letter to Pope Lucius (d.254), who had recently returned from banishment, he reminds him of how the three youths in the fiery furnace and Daniel in the lions' den were protected but survived, still retaining their dignity. 'Martyrdoms deferred do not diminish the merits of confession, but show forth the greatness of divine protection' (*Epistle* 57.2). Nonetheless, Cyprian does not eschew the merits of martyrdom. He acknowledges the precariousness of the Christians' position in an empire that demands religious obedience as a way of unifying disparate peoples: 'We are still placed in the battlefield. We fight daily for our lives' (*Epistle* 6.2). A number of his other letters aim to encourage those 'confessors' in prison or facing martyrdom: 'Let no one think of death, but of immortality; nor of temporary punishment, but of eternal glory' (*Epistle* 80.2). Cyprian himself, even though he was criticized for fleeing to avoid persecution (249–51), would ultimately embrace martyrdom for his faith.

## Martyrdom as 'media asset'

Several accounts of martyrdoms have survived because the early church historian Eusebius of Caesarea made them an integral part of his written works, the *Church History* being the most significant. In an original interpretation Doron Mendels (in *The Media Revolution of Early Christianity*) draws on the contemporary tools of media theory to suggest that for Eusebius martyrdom was a 'media asset'. Analysing Eusebius's collection of edited martyr stories, Mendels suggests that martyrdom presented the church with a 'golden opportunity to advertise itself' in the public sphere. Eusebius uses these skilfully selected 'publicity' stories to highlight how Christian endurance in the face of extreme suffering was persuasive to the watching audiences. It would have been a shock to audiences who prized the body and were used to seeing the violent strength of the gladiators, to see people who embodied the belief that the preservation of the *sarx* (flesh) was nothing compared to the valuing of the *pneuma* (spirit). At times, Mendels' almost exclusive use of the language of media theory jars as an interpretative tool for understanding Eusebius and the resistance embodied by the martyrs. Nevertheless, he rightly highlights how Eusebius selects, edits, and adapts to create a series of striking narratives.

One of the earliest accounts of a Christian martyrdom outside the New Testament is in a letter quoted by Eusebius (from the church at Smyrna to the church at Philomelium in Phrygia) detailing the death of Bishop Polycarp. The precise date of this martyrdom is debated (*c*.155–9, 166–7, or 177). Probably written soon after the event, it famously describes how in the arena Polycarp looks out sternly on the crowd, waves his hand at them, groans, looks up to heaven, saying: 'Away with the Atheists'. He then refuses to 'revile Christ', declaring: '86 years have I served Christ and he has done me no injury' (*Ecclesiastical History* 4.15.19–20). The crowd's demand that a lion be let loose on him was turned down as the games were already closed, so he was burnt at the stake, praying to God that he might 'share in the cup of Christ'. To an even greater extent than Stephen, Polycarp's martyrdom is paralleled to Christ's passion. Like many other early Christian martyrs, Polycarp is shown to be following in the footsteps of Christ.

In what reads like a fictitious emendation to the account, demonstrating Polycarp's sanctity, he is protected from the fire and instead stabbed to death, at which point his gushing blood quenches the flames. Throughout the ordeal he is depicted as being totally in control of his body, his emotions, and any residual fear. In this case the body was the site of a profoundly public struggle. It was as if the state was attempting to inscribe its power over the martyr's body, while through his dignified and semi-miraculous death he was able to resist this ideological inscription. In other words, the account of Eusebius depicts Polycarp's aged body as a site of resistance. Like many early martyrs, he appears to have decided to use the opportunity to address the crowd.

## Martyrdom and spectacle

Eusebius had a good eye for selecting spectacular dramas. He quotes, apparently verbatim, a letter by the Christians of Lyons and Vienne in Gaul to the Christians in Asia and Phrygia, describing the torture and martyrdom of at least forty-eight Christians in 177. The letter describes how, following social sanctions, castigation by a mob, imprisonment, torture, and legal examination, several Christians were led forth to the wild beasts. Mauled by the animals, shouted at by the crowds, and roasted on the iron chair, Maturus and Sanctus survived until they were finally 'sacrificed, having been made a spectacle to the world throughout that day as a substitute for all the variations of gladiatorial contests' (*Ecclesiastical History* 5.1.38–40). Executing Christians was a significantly cheaper form of entertainment than gladiators, and in certain cities it appears to have been used to reduce the costs of the games.

Another from the group was Blandina who continued to pray even as she was impaled 'hung on a stake and offered as a prey to the wild beasts that were let in'. To the Christian spectators and survivors this appeared like hanging on a cross. The wild beasts would not attack her and she was removed for another day of entertainment. It was not until the last day of the gladiatorial sports that Blandina, accompanied by Ponticus, a 15-year-old boy, returned to the arena, and there 'after scourging, after the beasts, after the gridiron, she was at last put in a net and thrown to a bull. She was tossed about a long time by the beast...until she too was sacrificed, and the heathen themselves confessed that never before among them had a woman suffered so much and so long' (*Ecclesiastical History* 5.1.56). Certain critics consider that such graphic retelling represents a pornography of death; for others it is a sensational device used by Eusebius to show how Blandina is depicted as a still point in the midst of the sound and fury of the arena. Blandina may have been only a weak slave girl, but she is celebrated as a 'noble athlete' who endured, and a gladiator who was successful in combat. Both metaphors recur in several other descriptions of early Christian martyrdoms. She is masculinized, portrayed as displaying what were perceived as masculine fighting qualities, without actually becoming a man. Her endurance is closely linked with Christ's crucifixion. Her martyrdom is offered as a counter-spectacle to the public violence of the games, as well as a battle against 'the evil one'. This is portrayed not only as an earthly spectacle but also as part of a cosmic spectacle.

## Perpetua's *Passion*

Perpetua's martyrdom in the arena is one well-known example of how the Roman state employed public violence as a form of entertainment, in an attempt to encourage loyalty to the apparent bringer of peace, the emperor. Vibia Perpetua was about 22 years old when she was arrested, tried, and imprisoned. Along with several companions, she was put to death in Carthage's arena on 7 March 203, as a sacrifice marking the birthday of Geta, the youngest son of the emperor Septimus Severus (145–211). Perpetua was an educated married woman from a reasonably wealthy family who was still breast-feeding her infant son. Her parents were still alive and one of her two brothers was also a catechumen (someone being trained and instructed in preparation for baptism). There is no mention of her husband in the accounts we have today. Her crime was to refuse to make a sacrifice to the emperor. This was an act of civil disobedience. Refusal to offer a sacrifice for the emperor's health and safety was seen as an act of treason. The previous year, Emperor Septimus Severus had issued a decree that prohibited conversion to Christianity or Judaism. Carthage's proconsul, Publius Aelius Hilarianus, appears to have followed this new imperial edict zealously.

Along with Perpetua, a number of other young catechumens, including Revocatus and his fellow slaves Felicitas, Saturninus, and Secundulus were condemned to 'fight with the beasts of the arena'. Chapters 3 to 10 of *Passio Perpetuae et Felicitatis*, which has survived in both Latin and Greek, are generally accepted to be by Perpetua herself and to represent an evocative description of resistance to the demands of the state prior to the spectacles of death. Unlike other *Passions* and the author of the narrative who describes her final moments in the arena, Perpetua does not attempt to make her story exemplary, preferring instead to concentrate on the particular details of her own experience, such as refusing her father's repeated appeals to change her mind, worrying about looking after her baby son, and relief that her breasts have not become engorged after her separation from him. Unlike the story of Blandina's death, which assumes the perspective of a male, almost sadistic, gaze at her violent death, Perpetua's staccato first-person account of her arrest, trial, and visions in prison provide a compelling insight into the human cost of resisting the power of the state.

This autobiographical prison diary sheds light on her visions or dreams. In her final vision, 'the day before our fight', she is met at the prison gate by Pomponius the deacon. He takes her by the hand, along 'rough winding ways', and they arrive at the amphitheatre 'breathless', and she is then taken into the middle of the arena. As the vision continues he reassures her: 'Don't be afraid; here I am, beside you, sharing your toil.' He disappears and she sees 'the immense, astonished crowd'. As she prepares to fight against an Egyptian of 'foul aspect' a giant purple-robed man appears who is even taller than the amphitheatre. His sandals are made of gold and silver and he carries a baton like the judge at a gladiatorial fight or athletic contest. He declares what will happen if either wins and then draws back. Perpetua and the Egyptian fight: he tries to grab her feet, but she strikes him in the face with her heels. After more fighting she treads on his head, much to the delight of her supporters. Triumphant, she receives a green bough laden with apples (probably symbolizing the immortal apples of Greek myth which are guarded by nymphs known as the Hesperides). The judge gives them to her saying, 'Daughter, peace be with you!' She heads towards the Gate of the Living (*Porta Sanavivaria*) out of the arena and then awakens.

This vision reflects some of the inner turmoil apparent in Perpetua's psyche prior to her actual appearance in Carthage's amphitheatre, which, located on the north-western edge of the city, was second in size only to the Colosseum and probably able to seat about 30,000 people. The conflicts in her dreams suggest that there was real anxiety coursing beneath the surface about what was about to happen to her, and whether she would be strong enough to hold to her convictions. Like her other dreams, which she describes earlier in her diary, it ends peacefully, and from the way her account concludes she sounds resolved to face the ordeal ahead. The language of this vision also appears to echo parts of the fifth chapter of the Song of Songs, which suggests that Perpetua's dreaming may have been influenced by this love poem, which was interpreted mystically by early Christians. The loving and frightening aspects of the Song of Songs passage are also manifested in Perpetua's vision. Several scholars have gone even further, suggesting that the purple-robed figure is to be identified not as her father, nor as Pomponius transformed, but as Christ who provides spectacles that serve the will of God. This may partly be a rhetorical device to encourage Christians facing martyrdom to be brave, but, nevertheless, from this perspective the martyrdoms at the games are transformed from being controlled by the local magistrate or governor to being overseen by God. This insight underlines a paradox at the heart of early Christian engagement with and remembering of the *munera* (the games). The dominant motif is trenchant criticism and resistance towards the games, while a less common theologically determined interpretation is to see them as being used and ultimately controlled by God.

The practice of the martyrs, many of them women like Perpetua, has recently led to critical discussions relating to gender and martyrdom. It is claimed by some scholars that the way in which some martyrdom narratives emphasize the weakness of women and the priority of male church leaders reflects the power of the male gaze over these subjects. The unexpected visions and original insights of Perpetua remain a refreshing corrective to the male layers of interpretation of her experience.

## The motives of martyrdom

The motives behind many martyrs' actions are hard to discern precisely across the 'ugly ditch' of history. Why did Perpetua embrace martyrdom? Was it belief in a crucified or martyred God, expectation of rewards in the afterlife, as well as loyalty to friends and commitment to the wider Christian community? Her steadfastness in prison and then in the arena may well have also been influenced by the Carthaginian tradition of self-sacrifice and suicide, which while it was discouraged by the Roman authorities continued to exert a considerable influence over the popular imagination. This was also perhaps fed by her reading of romantic novels that described the young taking independent and brave actions.

Another element was the rituals, practices, and social interactions within the Christian community that she had recently entered. At the time of her arrest Perpetua was a catechumen, and thus not a fully fledged member of the church, but her baptism while under house arrest was a serious statement of intent, even of resistance. Barring her rescinding and making a sacrifice to the emperor it appears to have almost guaranteed her own death in the arena. Not long after Perpetua's death, her martyrdom was incorporated into the evolving collective memory, which helped to define the identity of the early Christian community. Early Christian theologies of martyrdom are rooted in the belief that the martyrs such as Perpetua, Blandina, and Polycarp were imitating Christ, moving through suffering and death to life and victory.

## Martyrdom's spectators

For the organizers, often known as the *editores*, of the games, the passivity of Christians in the face of the violence directed against them in the amphitheatre became a problem. Part of the reason for this was that spectators had certain expectations as to the usual ordering, style, and form of public executions. Audiences expected to see the power of the state overwhelm the bodies of the condemned. They came to witness the victims shaking with terror, crying, or urinating out of fear as the beasts were released or other brutal types of execution were deployed against them. It appears that some Christians gave way, following this expected script. For example, Quintus from Phrygia, according to the letter describing Polycarp's martyrdom, when he 'saw the beasts and the other threats', was 'overcome in his mind and weakened and finally abandoned his salvation' (*Ecclesiastical History* 4.15.7). Other Christians were more resilient, shattering audience expectations, masking their emotions, and shunning the body language of understandable fear. In this way martyrdoms subverted Roman spectacles.

Audience responses were mixed. Many spectators were disappointed, frustrated, and sometimes made furious by the way in which some Christians would not fit into the usual pattern of the games, defying the authority of the presiding officials, as well as accepting torture and death without the usual symptoms of terror. The evidence for these claims needs to be handled with care as the *passiones* or *martyria*, the accounts of the last days and death of the martyrs, have undergone adaptation and editing. Some descriptions clearly romanticize the events, transforming the martyrs into early Christian saints with supernatural powers over the beasts, the fires, and their gladiatorial executioners. Nonetheless, the written records of the early pre-Constantinian martyrdoms can be seen to include significant elements of original material, and so long as these accounts are read critically, they can still shed some light on the actions of early Christians. The cumulative evidence from these 'passions' shows how both the speech and the body language of martyrs often communicated an acceptance of death.

It appears that seeing 'the blood of the martyrs' spilt (see Tertullian, *The Apology* 50) planted a seed in some imaginations. Justin Martyr, for example, appears to have been drawn to Christianity by seeing martyrs die: 'I watched them stand fearless in the face of death and of every other thing that was considered dreadful'

(*Second Apology* 12). It was bemusing for some viewers to be confronted by the early Christians' willingness to die for their beliefs. Justin, often described as the first Christian philosopher, was himself beheaded (*c.*165) during the reign of the emperor Marcus Aurelius (121–80) for his beliefs and refusing to sacrifice to the gods. Many early Christians perceived martyrs such as Justin as following in the footsteps of Jesus Christ, inspired by the Holy Spirit, and assured of immediate access to heaven. While early Christian martyrs appear to have inspired admiration, conversion, and even devotion, they also provoked annoyance, anxiety, and even loathing.

In many *passiones*, or accounts of martyrdoms, the words and actions of the individual peaceful martyrs stand in sharp contrast to the crowd, who are frequently portrayed as an unruly mob, baying for the blood of the Christians. Emboldened viewers could be cruel, mocking the *damnati ad bestias* as they were fatally mauled. For example, one of Perpetua's companions, Saturus, is bitten by a leopard in the arena, so drenching him with blood that as he came away the mob roared in witness to his second baptism: 'Well washed! Well washed!' This has been interpreted as an ironic inversion of a common phrase from the Roman baths *Saluum lotum* (well washed) or an exclamation taken from a Carthaginian sacrificial ritual. At this distance it is impossible to be sure what was in the minds of the spectators as they shouted this phrase at Saturus, but the narrator and probable eyewitness reinterprets this phrase in terms of baptism: 'For well washed indeed was one who had been bathed in this manner.' This affirmation reflects the common admiration, and later veneration, that martyrs received from the early Christian communities.

This experience of the games, combined with exhortations from the likes of the North African theologian Tertullian (*c.*160–225) do not appear, however, to have prevented some Christians from watching the games or specifically witnessing martyrdoms in the arena. The frequency with which many early theologians highlighted the idolatrous nature of activities in the amphitheatre suggests that many Christians were not persuaded to reject the games (*munera*) in theory or practice. According to the letter describing the martyrdom of Montanus and Lucius in the mid 3rd century, many Christians were present, watching and even learning how to die as martyrs. The implication here is that this practice of viewing had been going on for some time. Given the number and range of apparent eyewitness accounts, it appears that members of early Christian communities were not deterred from attending, showing solidarity, listening to the final speeches, indulging voyeuristically, attempting to claim the corpses, and writing up the events for posterity. Their records have ensured that some martyrs are commemorated, even venerated, up to the present day.

About fifty years after Perpetua's martyrdom in the mid-250s, there was a dramatic shift in official policy away from highly public executions, which gave martyrs the opportunity to turn their resistance into a 'media event' in the public sphere. Governors no longer provided Christians with a public theatre to play out their faith, preferring to execute them quietly, away from the arena. Cyprian of Carthage (d.258), for example, was beheaded not in the amphitheatre in front of a large crowd, but at a private villa where the proconsul was relaxing. This change in policy does not appear to have undermined at least some Christians' resolve in the face of empire-wide persecutions. Nor did it temper the desire of other early Christians to preserve the memory of martyrs, if not also their bodies. It contributed, in fact, to the development of sites of burial, with permanent memorials to those who had died in the faith.

## Communal martyrdoms

People like Polycarp, Blandina, and Perpetua did not act as isolated individuals. As members of small Christian communities and local congregations, they found encouragement, support, and ultimately eyewitnesses to their suffering and martyrdoms.

While some early Christian writers employed the metaphor of training or enduring like a gladiator, it was invariably towards a different and more peaceful end. Given the recurring divisions among Christian communities in North Africa, it is unrealistic to claim that such martyrdoms brought about harmony or unity. Nonetheless, it is striking to see how the non-violent resistance of martyrs, emerging out of local Christian communities, stands in sharp contrast to the practised, trained, violent performance of arena fighters that was honed in gladiatorial schools. There was one point of similarity, which would probably have surprised many spectators: some martyrs met their deaths like highly trained gladiators, with dignified restraint.

The change of Christianity's status from a persecuted sect to becoming, first, decriminalized in 311, then recognized as one of the Roman religions following the Edict of Milan in 313, and finally being made the official religion of the empire in 391 (by Emperor Theodosius) led to the end of imperial persecutions. It was several generations before the games ended, even after the emperor Constantine (272–337) prohibited them on 1 October 325. Combats in the arena continued, in various forms, until 404, when Honorius finally abolished them altogether. This was prompted, according to Theodoret of Cyrus's (c.393–c.457) church history, by the murder and martyrdom of a monk, Telemachus. He had entered the arena in an endeavour to stop the fight, but the 'spectators of the slaughter were indignant' and 'stoned the peacemaker to death'. In some parts of the empire games probably continued a little beyond this event, with medallions produced as late as the 430s or 440s depicting gladiators in combat, some even celebrating the return of *munera*. The races at the circus would continue for many generations. In a sermon around 440 Pope Leo the Great complained that the people of Rome preferred to go to the circus than attend church: 'mad spectacles draw greater crowds than blessed martyrdoms' (Sermon 84).

Nevertheless, before the end of the 4th century Christian communities were no longer the focal point for persecution. In this context martyrdom was increasingly spiritualized. Some leaders encouraged Christians to search for new kinds of martyrdom, for example embracing a life of asceticism, marked out by actions such as extreme fasting, sleepless vigils, and the wearing of hair shirts. These were some of the ways of 'mortifying' or 'martyring' the flesh. The theologian Athanasius (*c.*296–373) celebrated the hermit and monk Anthony's 'daily' martyrdoms in his *Life of Anthony* (*c.*360). As an alternative to martyrdom in the arena, some Christians sought martyrdom in the desert, while others eagerly attempted to become martyrs through provoking the wrath of pagan neighbours. Some monks appear to have turned violently against possible persecutors. Other Christians even became persecutors for the state against perceived 'heretics'. For example, schismatic Christian groups such as the North African Donatists were persecuted between 316 and 321, as well as during the early 5th century and faced 'disciplinary violence' and even 'martyrdom' under the Christian Roman Empire.

We have seen how up to Constantine's reign some early Christians became inextricably involved with the games, not by brandishing a sword but rather by becoming a victim. This resulted not in a gladiatorial triumph but in a series of public deaths, which to those outside the Christian community might have appeared meaningless, scandalous, and perplexing. The victims themselves, their fellow believers, and early Christian writers (like the theologian Tertullian), editors, and historians (like Eusebius) developed distinctive ways of anticipating, describing, and remembering martyrdom. Some post-Constantinian accounts became more sensational, eroticized, and elaborate as they were further removed from the original events. Increasingly, terse martyr *Acts* became supplanted by more elaborate martyr *Legends*.

Both before and after Constantine's reign, stories about martyrdom were turned into what Elizabeth Castelli describes in her book on

*Martyrdom and Memory* as a 'usable past' and part of a 'living tradition'. Sometimes Greek stories about Socrates' death or Jewish stories about the Maccabean martyrs were drawn upon to celebrate subsequent martyrdoms. Currently there is lively scholarly debate as to whether early Christians primarily or even exclusively drew upon Jewish roots or Graeco-Roman traditions. It appears that different Christian communities drew upon different traditions. In other words, some writers and preachers interpreted martyrdoms as standing in the earlier Greek and Roman 'noble death' traditions, while many others turned to the Jewish 'voluntary violent death' traditions. The two traditions were sometimes merged. In many cases this memorialization went even further. Martyrs became noble heroes to be elevated. Both early (pre-391) and later (post-391) accounts turned what were often agonizing deaths into events to be remembered, repeated, and celebrated. The result is that many of these stories of martyrdom continue to reverberate hundreds of years after they were first told.

# Chapter 4
# **Contesting martyrdom**

Up to this point we have seen how stories about martyrdom are used in both Jewish and Christian traditions. It is clear that 'martyrdom' is not a stable term with a single meaning. This is also the case within Islamic traditions. New communication technologies have contributed to this instability, as well as to the preservation and circulation of both ancient and more recent stories about martyrdom. Over the last few years martyrdom has gone digital. The digitization of martyrdom is changing the ways martyrs are commemorated, remembered, and interpreted. Audiences now have direct access to countless original martyrdom stories, texts, and martyrologies (lists of martyrs). Online images of both ancient and modern martyrs are now widely accessible. A few taps on a computer or mobile phone and anyone can see the faces of those named as martyrs. They criss-cross the globe, weaving unexpected patterns, leaving traces of deaths that otherwise might be forgotten.

In the last decade websites, blogs, and Facebook pages have been established to commemorate martyrs and their martyrdoms. Video sites such as YouTube commonly highlight the lives and provide details of the deaths of martyrs. Different approaches are taken. Some focus on a single martyr, others on commemorating a whole cluster of martyrdoms. Some celebrate historic martyrs, while others highlight more recent deaths. These digital processes have contributed to the contests that commonly cluster around martyrdom stories. This can be seen not only in Jewish and Christian traditions, discussed in the previous two chapters, but also in debates concerning martyrdom within Islamic traditions.

## Commemorating martyrdom

Like many other Middle Eastern countries, Syria has a layered martyrdom tradition. Recent deaths are adding to a long history of commemorating martyrdom. While the sites and web pages publicizing recent martyrs in Syria have become points of protest, debate, and contest, other online Syrian sites appear to provoke less debate. They do, however, illustrate how the memories of martyrs and martyrdoms can be preserved and used in an attempt to draw together a nation, while others can be used to underline how a nation is divided.

For example, a short home-made high-definition film entitled *Martyrs Gallery for Syria* (11 December 2011) uploaded to YouTube begins with mundane footage: pedestrians walk by an illuminated Christmas tree in Trafalgar Square and along the pavement in front of the National Gallery in London. This is followed by a montage of about 12 still images, showing over 30 small stands, each with a photograph on the back and front. The camera acts like a guide, taking the viewer from one stand to another. A melancholic mix of piano and synthesized violin music accompanies the film and the viewer. Next to each photograph is a short résumé against the backdrop of a Syrian flag, too faint to read on the video. On the film subtitles below several of the faces give their names and ages. A candle has been placed on the rain-swept pavement below one of the photographs. To an outsider they are simply a series of faces, with a few red, yellow, and white roses adorning the boards. They stare innocently out at each viewer. No one martyr or martyrdom is highlighted above another. Each martyr is given the same amount of space. There is equality in these representations of the departed. Only after a third viewing does one of the faces stand out: a chubby, friendly faced, blue-shirted boy with dark hair. The subtitle simply reads: 'Hamza Al-Kateeb—13 years old. Date of Martyrdom 24/05/2011.'

Why does Hamza's face emerge from the screen? He looks familiar. His photograph can be found on many other sites and on the front of several newspapers, from the middle of 2011. Photographs of his face and bruised body were used in demonstrations, against the Syrian government's harsh crackdown on protestors, all over the world. In both Istanbul and Beirut children held posters and photographs of this 13-year-old, along with protest signs and Syrian flags (Figure 5). Emblazoned in English on several was the simple call: 'Free Syria.' The *Martyrs Gallery for Syria* caught on camera nearly a dozen demonstrators waving Syrian flags among these martyr memorials in the pedestrian space near Trafalgar Square. These commemorative pictures continue to circulate online.

5. Syrian children carry pictures of 13-year-old Hamza al-Khatib, photograph 2011

Why is it that Hamza Al-Kateeb's name and story, among so many, was singled out? Answering this question sheds light on the broader processes behind the making of martyrs and why commemorating martyrdom can so often provoke contentious debates. His death became like a snowball tumbling down a mountain of publicity, attracting more and more attention. Several reports describe how the local police detained Hamza, along with other protestors, on 29 April 2011, and it wasn't until nearly a month later (on 27 May), that his mutilated body was returned to his parents. Another YouTube video shows his funeral, along with crowds holding his photo and a sign proclaiming: 'The martyr Hamza al-Khatib, killed under torture by Assad's gangs.' After the news agency Al Jazeera's Arabic service covered this story, replaying part of the video from his funeral alongside other images and comments, Hamza's story began to circulate both within and beyond the Middle East. Like other figures from earlier stages of the Arab Spring, such as Khaled Said in Egypt and Mohamed Bouazizi in Tunisia, stories about his death were turned into a symbol of the wider protest movement. Several Facebook pages were established to commemorate his death. The Arabic Facebook page, roughly translated as 'We are all the child martyr Hamza Alkhateeb', has over 500,000 followers. There are posts, discussions, and updates. It commemorates other more recent deaths, described as martyrdoms. Several people have posted videos of other funerals or pictures of Syrian martyrs on this site. In the days following news of his death in custody and the circulation of his mutilated figure, his death became a common talking point in many parts of Syria.

The claims that Hamza was a martyr and that he was tortured have been contested in several settings. For example, the Syrian state channel broadcast a sixty-minute programme about Hamza's death. Doctors were interviewed to support the claim that the injuries to his body, such as the burn marks and bruising, were not 'signs of torture' as some have claimed, but were 'faked by conspirators'. According to the programme, this deception was designed to try to incite the Syrian people to revolt. Parallels were drawn with how the people of Tunisia were motivated to revolt against the government following the self-immolation of the street vendor Bouazizi on 17 December 2010. This had led to the end of twenty-three years of rule by President Zine el-Abidine and many see it as the start of the Arab Spring. That state television contested the popular account of Hamza's death that was circulating online and around the world, and devoted so much airtime to refuting this story, implies that the Syrian government took news about this martyrdom extremely seriously.

Hamza's killing and torture became like a metonym, a single instance that illustrates a wider phenomenon in Syria. Some commemorative sites or pages that do not focus on a single martyrdom or martyr appear to attract smaller followings. For instance, 'We Are All Martyrs Of Syria (Syrian Revolution 2011)' on Facebook had under 100 followers in late 2011. Nevertheless, their aims resonate with many other similar sites: 'Our aim is to build a community of awareness so that Syrian martyrs will not be forgotten and their blood not lost.' Some sites show victim after victim, 'martyr' after 'martyr'. These bruised bodies and bloodied faces do not make for easy viewing. The desire to document gross human rights abuses and the killing of innocent civilians is the stated aim of many Arabic and English-language sites, such as 'Children Martyrs in Syria'. It is emotionally challenging, revealing picture after picture of children's faces, some dead or disfigured, combined with a lyrical song, which includes the refrain 'Tell me why does it have to be like this'. Captions add pleas for 'Help' and in slightly elusive English statements such as 'The blood of the children of the martyrs will not be wasted'. The recurring theme of these sites is that to remember and to commemorate these martyrdoms will help to ensure that their deaths are not in vain.

This practice is not restricted to cyberspace. For instance, in both Syria and Lebanon a national holiday called Martyrs' Day is celebrated on 6 May. This commemorates the execution of nationalists by Ottoman troops in both Damascus and Beirut back in 1916. The locations of their killings, in the centre of these two historic cities, have both been renamed Martyrs' Square. Travel around the Middle East and it is striking how many other cities and towns have squares, streets, and bridges named after martyrs. There are well-known Martyrs' Squares in Baghdad, Tripoli, and Egypt's Port Said, as well as in Palestinian towns such as Hebron, Nablus, and Hamle. Some have been recently renamed, while others have been in place for many decades. There is invariably a story attached to each location. Following the American attack on insurgents in Fallujah, Iraq in 2004, a football pitch was transformed into a place where as many as 500 local fighters were buried. Now known as the Martyrs' Cemetery, it has a sign outside that says: 'This cemetery is given by the people of Fallujah to the heroic martyrs of the battle against the Americans.' Even the road leading up to the cemetery has been renamed Martyrs' Cemetery Road.

It is Iran, however, that probably has the highest number of Martyrs' Squares. You can walk around them not only in the well-known cities of Tehran, Shariz, and Qum, but also in the less commonly visited centres of Arak, Gorgan, Kerman, Rasht, and Tabriz. Mashhad has a Martyrs' Square commemorating Ali al-Ridha (765–818). He is also known as Imam Riza, and is believed by Shi'a scholars to have been killed by his half-brother using poisoned grapes. The vast majority of these squares, however, were named as commemorative spaces for martyrs from either the 1979 Revolution or the 1980–88 Iran–Iraq War.

## Protesting martyrdom

If physical commemorative spaces can be sites of contest over martyrdom, so too can virtual digital spaces. One of the best known and widely discussed online martyrdom videos is the death of a 27-year-old Iranian woman, Neda Agha-Soltan. She was shot in the chest during a protest in Tehran on 20 June 2009. Her fiancé

Caspan Makan, told BBC Persian TV: 'She was near the area (of the demonstration), a few streets away, from where the main protests were taking place, near the Amir-Abad area. She was with her music teacher, sitting in a car and stuck in traffic. She was feeling very tired and very hot. She got out of the car for just for a few minutes. And that's when it all happened' (BBC News, 22 June 2009). Two bystanders caught her last moments on film. These images were posted on YouTube and other sites within a few hours of her death. They have since been watched by hundreds of thousands of viewers. Her death is sometimes used to highlight how after the presidential elections in 2009 thousands of protestors took to the streets in Tehran to challenge the final outcome. Soldiers, police, and militia on motorbikes, often wielding batons or clubs, suppressed these demonstrators more and more aggressively.

Only a few days after her death, anti-government demonstrators were waving enlarged photographs of Neda's face (Figure 6). The words 'I am Neda' were commonly printed across or below the picture of her blood-spattered face. This was used by protestors not only in Iran but around the globe. On several video sites images of her final moments were set to music. International news organizations either showed pictures of her bloodied face or repeated this disturbing amateur footage in documentaries such as *Neda: An Iranian Martyr* (BBC 24 November 2009). This documentary offered more insights into her life, her death, and the politically divided context in which she had died. In a similar fashion to young Hamza in Syria, following her death, memorial sites have been established and publicized through Facebook, Twitter, and Wikipedia. While some asserted she had become the martyr of a 'new revolutionary movement in Iran', others described her as the 'first YouTube martyr'.

In many ways Neda's death is a very different kind of martyrdom from many of the others considered in this book. Several news reports explained that she was a peaceful observer who had only

6. **Protester holding a portrait of Neda Agha-Soltan at a demonstration following the Iranian election results, during the G8 Foreign Minsters' Summit meeting in Trieste, Italy, on 25 June 2009**

stepped out of her friend's car for a breath of air. Neda did not intentionally seek martyrdom: she could be described as a passive or involuntary martyr. She was not involved in the protests; she did not die voluntarily or allow herself to be killed. She did not choose to die: her martyrdom was accidental.

Nevertheless, in just a few weeks her unintentional death was transformed into a digital, globally recognized martyrdom. The fact that her picture was used as a sign of protest both in Iran and in many other countries around the world underlines how politically charged some deaths can become. President Mahmoud Ahmadinejad questioned who had actually shot her. In one interview he even implied that it was part of a devious foreign plot by 'enemies of the state' to shame the nation. Neda is by no means the only Iranian whose death has led to competing claims and counter-claims.

For some the story of Neda's death will not only be amplified and regularly reiterated; it will also be elaborated and, given the confusing and contested circumstances, endlessly debated. These reverberations are already to be found in countless sites on the World Wide Web. Her end, like Hamza's, is used to promote a cause. The highly emotive debates around this kind of digital commemoration reflect the symbolic power of various kinds of martyrdom. Why is it that pictures and stories portraying martyrdom often carry such persuasive power?

## Founding martyrdoms

To answer such questions we have to go back many centuries before the advent of the printing press, let alone the development of the Internet, to 10 Moharram 680 when the Prophet Muhammad's grandson, Husayn, was captured, tortured, and killed by the caliph Yizad's soldiers. It is believed that his corpse was then decapitated. This took place at Karbala, which is now an Iraqi town about fifty miles south of Baghdad. While the murder of his father, Ali, is commemorated, it is Husayn's death that is commonly seen within Shi'ite Islam as the founding death. Some even suggest that the 'martyrdom of Husayn is to Shi'ites what the crucifixion is to Christians'. This suggestion may overlook the distinctiveness of the religious traditions, but for many Iranians Husayn's death over 1,300 years ago at Karbala has come to be seen as the 'supreme self-sacrifice'. After the life of the Prophet, this is the defining story of Shi'ism. Many Shi'ite Muslims see Husayn's death at Karbala as a pivotal moment in world history: an event that demands attention, reflection, and imitation. It sheds new light on suffering and martyrdom.

The significance and meaning of Husayn's death in 680 is contested both within and beyond Shi'ite Islam. This is also the case within the Sunni Islamic tradition. A wide range of texts retell the story of Karbala. These texts are regularly read, recited, and enacted in public. One of the most influential within Shi'ite Islam is Husayn Wa'iz Kashifi's book *Meadow of the Martyrs* (*Rawdat al-Shuhada*, c.1502). Using both poetry and prose, this text portrays individual and intimate scenes of martyrdom that are full of pathos. For example, Husayn finds his son Ali Akbar unconscious and covered in blood and dust. Dismounting, he lays his hand on his son's forehead, who awakens and in his dying words describes a vision of the Prophet holding two 'bowls of heavenly drink'. He is given one, but when he asks for another, because he is 'extremely thirsty', he is met with this reply: 'Ali! Drink only this one: I have reserved the other one for your father [Husayn]. He too will join me with blistered lips and bloody heart.' In the story this prediction comes true in Husayn's martyrdom, which is portrayed in detail. For many Shi'ite Muslims his death is not something to contest but rather something to celebrate and to commemorate.

Husayn's role appears to have evolved over the centuries within Shi'ite Islam, changing from that of devout intercessor to revolutionary example who resists unjust rulers. For some, this story provokes devotion, lamentation, and even physical self-harm. Why? For many these powerful emotional responses are part of annual public practices to atone for the fact that no assistance was sent to Husayn and his small band of seventy-two men when they were surrounded by enemies in the searing heat of the desert. In contrast to this comparatively passive pietism, his

51

story has more recently been used as an example of activism to emulate. Husayn is the model of a fighting brave martyr. This story was put to use before and during the 1979 revolutionary period in Iran and was therefore easily translatable into the eight-year conflict against Iraq that ensued. Some have even suggested that by following in Husayn's footsteps, 20th-century martyrs are helping to atone for the past sin of failing to offer assistance and even to prepare the way for the return of the Twelfth Imam.

Husayn is by no means the only martyr from an earlier age who is commemorated and celebrated in Iran. For example, Husayn's father, Ali, may have been the Prophet's cousin and son-in-law, but he was still murdered in the mosque of Kufa in 661. Ali's death is commemorated on the nineteenth night of Ramadan. At the very moment that he was entering the mosque at Kufa to perform morning prayer, an assassin from Egypt struck him on the head with a poisoned sword. Here was another betrayal and killing. It too was turned into a martyrdom to commemorate. In Iran, where over 90 per cent of the population are Shi'a, the stories relating to Karbala, especially the martyrdom of Husayn, and to a lesser extent the martyrdom of his father Ali and Husayn's son Ali Akbar, along with beliefs associated with the hidden Twelfth Imam (Muhammed Al-Mahdi), resonate in many people's imagination. This is partly because reference to these stories regularly found their way into public sermons, radio broadcasts, political speeches, university lectures, classroom lessons, and school textbooks. They continue to resonate today.

## Performing martyrdom

The events surrounding Husayn's martyrdom and his seventy-two companions' deaths are commonly re-enacted through colourful 'passion' plays (ta'ziya or ta'ziyeh). Ta'ziyeh can mean 'to mourn', 'to lament', or 'to share one another's grief'. These Persian passion commemorations originally emerged as a significant cultural force during the Safavid dynasty in the early 1500s and continue to attract large audiences (Figure 7). They commonly provoke strong emotional reactions from viewers. Some productions use professional actors, large casts of extras, and even live horses. Other more common plays are smaller in scale and produced by local all-male theatre companies for their own communities. Many of the adult actors have been involved in these plays since they were children. The story unfolds over several nights, each evening culminating in at least one death, though it is not usually until the final night of the performances that audiences see the martyrdom of Husayn. It is still possible to see these passion plays in many parts of Iran today. Dozens of them are also now available on sites such as YouTube.

In most Shi'ite villages, many flagellants process through the streets on the anniversary of Husayn's death, punishing themselves; they are acknowledging their culpability in his martyrdom. It is as if they are admitting that they too have betrayed the Prophet's grandson. In some processions women carry water as symbolic reminders of

7. *Ta'ziyeh* performance, Kermanshah, Iran, July 1999

how the Karbala martyrs suffered from agonising thirst and were prevented from reaching the Euphrates by Yazid's troops. In other processions some participants carry spades to act as a reminder that Husayn and his followers were initially left unburied. Husayn is widely referred to as 'Chief', 'Lord', or 'Prince of Martyrs', and his picture, along with one of his father Ali, is sometimes carried aloft in these processions.

Every year on Ashura, in some towns and cities mourners carry a heart-shaped wooden structure at the centre of the procession. This is covered with a black cloth, which at its centre has embroidered verses encircling a medallion in praise of Imam Husayn. Described as a *nakhl* (literally translated as 'palm tree') this symbolizes the coffin of Husayn. Pictures of Husayn and Ali can also be found in many graveyard cabinets of martyrs killed during the Iran–Iraq war. At least one mural from this time in Tehran shows a portrayal of Husayn holding an unnamed war martyr. What does it mean? That those who die as military martyrs will be rewarded in heaven and welcomed into the embrace of the 'Prince of Martyrs' himself, Imam Husayn.

## Preaching martyrdom

Martyrdom has played an important part in the speeches of revolutionary Iranian leaders such as Ruhollah Khomeini (1900–89), Sayyed Ali Khamenei (b.1939), and Akbar Rafsanjani (b.1934). These and other leaders repeatedly celebrated Husayn as a heroic war hero who bravely resisted 'tyranny' and strove 'for the preservation and revival of Islam'. In their sermons and speeches, the 1980–8 war is also depicted as a 're-enactment' of Husayn's martyrdom at Karbala. For some scholars such accounts stand in sharp contrast to earlier understandings of Husayn's martyrdom which perceived Husayn's death as a unique and unrepeatable sacrifice at one particular moment in history. Nevertheless, soldiers killed during the war were celebrated and portrayed by the leadership as following in the footsteps of Husayn. Martyrdom in *jihad* was glorified as 'the most certain way of receiving God's reward and obtaining a place in paradise'. Khomeini also proclaimed that martyrdom 'for the cause of God was…the ultimate perfection a human being could attain'.

Khomeini and other religious leaders (such as Ali Khameini, Khomeini's successor as supreme leader of Iran) regularly drew upon what some observers describe as the 'Karbala paradigm' in their sermons. For example, Khomeini said in one of his sermons: 'O Creator. Cause us to be among the people of Karbala.' To which his listeners replied 'Amen' (Friday prayers in Tehran, 13 October 1983). These homilies at the University of Tehran were broadcast by Iranian television and radio and also reproduced in books and newspapers. The post-revolutionary leaders of the Islamic republic frequently referred to Husayn's martyrdom and other events at Karbala in their addresses. They used such references to encourage the population to understand the value of martyrdom in the war, to promote particular kinds of ethical behaviour, and to reinforce their hold on power. While other deaths, such as those killed by Iraqi bombings in the cities, were described as 'martyrdoms', the highest honour or 'exaltation' was reserved for 'battlefield martyrs'. Murals, posters, and sermons celebrated the way 'blood can overcome the sword' and declared that 'to die a martyr is to pump blood into the veins of society'. These speeches, sermons, murals, and posters from the 1980s contributed to a communicative environment in which the idea of martyrdom became a central motivating force. The connection of contemporary martyrdom stories with sacred narratives enabled Iranian leaders to encourage others to join the war effort, and to show grieving relatives that the death of their son, father, or brother was not a meaningless waste in a seemingly endless war, but rather a religiously significant sacrifice.

Celebrating the death of martyrs has continued into the 21st century. For example, following the killings of several Iranian nuclear scientists in Iran during 2011 and 2012, Ayatollah

Khamenei told their relatives that these scientists were 'the elite martyrs', a 'source of honour for the country', and that their work 'made them' deserving of 'the honour of martyrdom in the path of Allah' (20 January 2012). This statement emerged online from the Office of the Supreme Leader Ayatollah Sayyed Ali Khamenei and reflects how martyrdom has continued to be used by political and religious leaders to honour the dead. It also highlights how local pronouncements about martyrdom can become internationalized through the World Wide Web.

## Depicting martyrdom

There are still several hundred murals in Iran commemorating soldiers who were killed during the Iran–Iraq War. Many were copied from smaller original posters or pictures. These images commonly connect the martyrdom of individual soldiers with the martyrdom of Husayn at Karbala. Others link the sacrificial death of a soldier with the leaders of the Islamic Revolution.

One of Iran's best-known depictions of a martyr is located near the main entrance of the University of Tehran. It is a huge mural painted on the side of a multistorey building. A serious-looking dark-haired boy stares out at passers-by, his youthfulness accentuated by the older bearded figure in the background, an easily recognizable portrayal of Ayatollah Khomeini. It is as if he is watching over the boy, while also looking beyond. Beneath Khomeini, in the foreground, several tanks point towards a single larger tank. During and after the war this 12-year-old boy soldier, Hossein Fahmideh, was turned into a national hero, celebrated for a very different reason from young Hamza in Syria.

One government account of his martyrdom describes how, without the knowledge of his parents, the youngster from Qom lied about his age in order to join the army. This was not unusual in a war that attracted thousands of boy soldiers, enthused by the vision of fighting together for their country and for God. What was exceptional was how he was killed. According to one official account, Hossein was fighting in the besieged southern city of Khorramshahr in November 1980. Seeing that many of his older colleagues had been killed, he took grenades from one of his dead comrades, clenched one to his body, and blew himself up beneath an Iraqi tank, disabling the tank and thereby halting an entire line of advancing tanks. Ayatollah Khomeini regularly celebrated Hossein's actions. On the pre-2009 mural Khomeini describes him as 'our guide' who 'threw himself under the enemy's tank with a grenade and destroyed it, thus drinking the elixir of martyrdom'.

Hossein's face appeared not only on murals, but also on banknotes, stamps, and stickers. Thousands of Iranian schoolchildren received plastic rucksacks adorned with a picture of his martyrdom. The story of his death, along with other ancient martyrdoms, was repeated in school textbooks aimed at improving literacy among children. His grave on the outskirts of Tehran was turned into a national monument, becoming a popular destination for pilgrimages. His story is still retold in speeches and news articles, leading some to describe him as the Islamic Revolution's 'grandson'. Around one million people were killed during the eight years of fighting, but while all Iranians killed during the fighting were seen as martyrs, Hossein was turned into a national celebrity partly because of his perceived youthful courage. The mural was repainted in 2009. While Hossein's face remains, it is now portrayed in front of a more abstract background of red, black, and orange waves in a dark frame among grey clouds. In place of Khomeini's face and the Iraqi tank, there is now a single grenade encircled by three candles.

This is one among many murals celebrating martyrdom to be found in Tehran and in other parts of Iran. While many people were responding to the losses of the Iran–Iraq war, some more recent ones celebrate Palestinian martyrdoms. Over the last few years several researchers have spoken with students and faculty at the University of Tehran about these murals, including that commemorating Hossein's martyrdom. Interestingly, many had not have even noticed it, while others saw it as part of Iran's past. Murals, posters, and sermons are by no means the only form of communication used to promote martyrdom. The Iranian government has sponsored both the production of 'sacred defence' films and more recently (since 2007) the creation of video games to celebrate martyrdom.

## Interpreting martyrdom

There are multiple interpretations of both the meaning and the value of martyrdom. These can be found expressed online, and in a range of documentary films. In the documentary *The Cult of the Suicide Bomber* (2005, Sean Batty and Kevin Toulis), the presenter Robert Baer begins his account of suicide bombing with the story of the 13-year-old Iranian, Hossein Fahmideh. In the film Baer visits the boy's highly adorned grave, at Behesht-e-Zahra cemetery in Tehran, and then the family of the boy who, like many in Iran, still see him as a hero. Baer sees a small shrine that the family preserve in memory of their teenage son. Hossein's family show him the rucksack with his photograph on, which was mass-produced and given to Iranian children. When he asks if Hossein was 'the first suicide bomber' Hossein's sister-in-law forcefully replies: 'He was a martyr. It is impossible to describe him as anything else. He was a martyr through and through.'

In Iran he may have been portrayed as a heroic soldier, but this documentary implies that he should be seen as a prototype suicide bomber. It then takes viewers from Hossein's story in the Iran–Iraq war to car bomb attacks on the American Embassy and marine barracks in Beirut, Lebanon (April 1983 and October 1983), via several attacks on buses in Jerusalem to bombings on the London Underground (July 2005). The documentary posits a clear evolutionary progress to the 'virus' of suicide bombing. The History Channel's *Inside the Mind of a Suicide Bomber* (2006, Tom

Roberts) does something similar, making a link between suicide bomb attacks in Israel and Lebanon in the last two decades with Japanese kamikaze pilots diving their planes into American ships in 1944 as part of an operation known as 'Divine Wind'.

Some films and online discussions fail to distinguish between the different political, religious, and cultural beliefs that motivate suicide bombers: it is simpler to draw all these motivations together. Robert Baer, in his article 'This Deadly Virus' in the *Observer* newspaper, claims that:

> Like all cults, the cult of suicide bombing feeds upon itself. Log on to the internet or visit a militant Islamic bookshop and within a few minutes you will find enough inspiration in CDs, ranting sermons, DVDs, for a hundred suicide bombs. It swirls across the Islamic world as an expression of rage against the West for the invasion of Iraq, support for Israel, and for Western dominance of the world economy...Amid the rage is the glorification of martyrdom. In a Gaza mosque I saw 'official certificates of martyrdom' being handed out like graduation diplomas to the families of suicide bombers. (7 August 2005)

Baer takes the reader in a single paragraph from a 'militant Islamic bookshop' to the whole 'Islamic world'. This blurring is common, and does not do full justice to the theological debates around martyrdom within Islam. The result is to create the sense of a storm of fierce anger against the West, articulated through the glorification of suicide attacks. He also underlines the wide variety of media that are used to promote suicide attacks as a part of the 'cult of martyrdom'. This has been and still is celebrated through posters, graffiti, audio cassettes, videos, and other kinds of street media in many towns and villages in the West Bank and Gaza.

Writers such as Mia Bloom, in *Dying to Kill: The Allure of Suicide Terror* (2005), and Robert Pape, in *Dying to Win: The Strategic Logic of Suicide Terrorism* (2005), have gone beyond purely theological or religious explanations for what motivates bombers. While some groups clearly hope to increase news coverage of their cause, attract new followers, inspire fear among the wider public, and even compete with other terrorist groups, there are other political goals. In the face of overwhelming force and power suicide attacks may be perceived as one of the few remaining options available to a comparatively weak organization. Pape draws upon his extensive database of suicide bombing and his reading of the history of suicide attacks, as well as the contemporary expressions of the current phenomenon to conclude that a suicide attack is an 'extreme strategy for national liberation' and therefore 'mainly a response to foreign occupation'.

This interpretation is contested both online and offline, with many posters emphasizing the religious roots and theological justifications of what are described not as 'suicide attacks' but rather as 'martyrdom operations' (*amaliyat istishhadiya*). While suicide is explicitly prohibited in Islam (Qur'an 2:195, 4:29), numerous websites express the view that 'self-sacrificing' acts or 'martyrdom operations' are justifiable in certain circumstances. Many different media, from books and pamphlets to television programmes and web pages, are employed to promote these and related perspectives. Attacks upon Iraqi Shi'as by Iraqi Sunnis may be critiqued through both Arabic and Western news reports, but on some websites they are justified and celebrated. In such contexts, these acts are sometimes interpreted as going beyond purely 'a response to a foreign occupation' to acts of religious obedience.

It is noteworthy that following the American invasion of Iraq in 2003, Shi'a celebrations leading up to the Ashura festival, which marks the anniversary of Hussein's death, have become a target for suicide bomb attacks, presumed to be carried out by Sunni radicals intent on inciting further divisions. Such attacks illustrate how certain radical Sunnis have also embraced martyrdom operations, which according to some scholars is a comparatively recent phenomenon within Sunni Islam. David Cook argues that beliefs about *Martyrdom in Islam* (2007) 'have evolved to suit prevailing circumstances'. He claims that, among certain Sunni and Shi'a communities, classical inclusive understandings of martyrdom, which also condemn suicide, have been replaced by a narrower perception of martyrdom.

## Debating martyrdom

While suicide attacks regularly receive vociferous support, as well as theological justification and redefinition as 'martyrdom operations', there are many examples on the Web of Muslims debating the appropriateness and legitimacy of suicide attacks, not only among clerics but also among the laity. Online there is a democratization of debates. Scholars or religious leaders no longer have a monopoly on textual interpretation. Passionately held theologies of martyrdom come into conflict. Following the attacks on the World Trade Center in New York in September 2001, there were diverse reactions within what Gary Bunt in *Islam in the Digital Age* describes as 'cyber Islamic environments', where a few extremists celebrated them as martyrdoms to be honoured as part of a broader *jihad* and striving for Allah, while many others unequivocally condemned them on religious grounds. As with every other diverse global religious tradition, rigorous discussions regularly take place on the Web, with participants drawing upon a range of translated Muslim scriptures and authorities. For example, the Egyptian Sunni scholar Yusuf al-Qaradawi, who himself issued a *fatwa* (a religious edict) about suicide bombing, is frequently cited on the Web as an authority for his support of suicide bombing in Palestine: 'Allah Almighty is just; through his infinite wisdom he has given the weak a weapon the strong do not have and that is their ability to turn their bodies into bombs as Palestinians do.'

Alongside such statements are contrasting voices, such as those found within a 23,000-word policy document entitled *The Hijacked*

*Caravan: Refuting Suicide Bombings as Martyrdom Operations in Contemporary Jihad Strategy.* This was produced by an Islamic think-tank known as Ihsanic Intelligence. It was published online a day after the attacks in London on 7 July 2005. They conclude uncompromisingly:

> The technique of suicide bombing is anathema, antithetical and abhorrent to Sunni Islam. It is considered legally forbidden, constituting a reprehensible innovation in the Islamic tradition, morally an enormity of sin combining suicide and murder and theologically an act which has consequences of eternal damnation.

Qaradawi's pronouncements and this contrasting report are significant because they illustrate that individual and independent Islamic interpretations are becoming increasingly common on the Web.

These kinds of online debates draw not only on texts, but also on images. In the aftermath of the London bombings, several websites were created. One of the most interesting was the Islamic site 'Not in the Name of Peace'. The site's creator was a young British Muslim, Muhammad Ridha Payne. His opening statement on the site is passionate: 'We need to show these maniacs that none of us think what they are doing is right, justified or Islamically based.' Payne believes that 'Islam has very clear guidelines as to what is right and what is wrong'. He acknowledges that: 'Of course we all feel aggrieved by actions in Afghanistan, Iraq and Palestine but this does not give anyone the right to kill further innocent people.'

Several pictures posted on this site showed people praying. For instance, above two men kneeling, their heads touching the prayer carpet of a mosque, were the words 'The proverb says "slaughter your ego with the dagger of self-discipline"'; below them three words were added: 'not slaughter people'. While this site appears to have been removed, the sentiments are far from unique.

On another site, a simple image of a road sign has been changed, along with a quotation from the '*The Holy Quran* (5:32)' in English: '...to kill one person is like killing the whole of mankind...And to give life to one person is like giving life to the whole of mankind.' Many of these images assert that 'true' Islam is a peaceful and life-bringing faith. In short, they are challenging predatory forms of martyrdom that aim to take other people's lives.

Even more common are detailed online textual debates on the significance and precise meaning of the words *shaheed* (martyr) and *istishhad* (martyrdom). *Shaheed* originally evolved from the Arabic term 'to witness' or 'to see', and is widely accepted as having links with the original Greek term and subsequent Latin usage. Nevertheless, the term has evolved and developed a range of social, legal, and religious meanings within different Islamic traditions. One of the most common interpretations is to see martyrdom as dying 'while striving in the path of God' ( *jihad*). This is often connected with being killed on the battlefield 'in God's cause', for Allah welcomes martyrs (see Qur'an 3:140). Many contributors to sites such as Ummah Forum affirm the common belief that the Qur'an bestows the highest status on those who die in battle: 'Do not think that those who were killed on the path of God are dead. They are alive and well provided for by their Lord' (3:169). These claims reflect a 9th-century development where *shaheed* came to refer predominantly to the 'military martyr', whose sins would be forgiven and who would automatically be admitted into Paradise.

This interpretation is debated, as it is pointed out that earlier traditions had a more expansive view of martyrdom. Once again foundational texts are used to support interpretation of this perspective, alongside everyday issues. On 4 February 2011, the blog entitled 'Islam Message of Peace' attempted to answer the question: 'Does a person who died of cancer as a result of smoking attain the status of a martyr?' In response, the companion of the Prophet Muhammad, Abu Hurayrah (603–81) is quoted, who recorded that according to the Prophet there are five kinds of martyrs: 'the one who dies of the plague, the one who dies of a stomach disease, the one who drowns, the one who is crushed beneath a falling wall, and the martyr who is killed for the sake of Allah'.

Another commonly quoted and closely related text, the *Al-Muwatta*, is from the founder of the Sunni Maliki school of law, Malik (d.795). In this tradition the title of *shaheed* is not restricted to only those who die on the battlefield. Seven other kinds of martyrs are recognized by the Prophet:

> He who dies as a victim of an epidemic is a martyr; he who dies from drowning is a martyr; he who dies from pleurisy is a martyr; he who dies from diarrhoea is a martyr; he who dies by [being burned in] fire is a martyr; he who dies by being struck by a dilapidated wall falling is a martyr; and the woman who dies in childbed is a martyr.

This broader view of martyrdom was gradually replaced by a belief in the priority of military martyrs. While the Web reveals how this understanding is not uncritically absorbed, many scholars endorse the belief that the concept of martyrdom has evolved within Islam. In spite of this both the Qur'an and the Hadith have become locations for open online contest, as different groups seek to promote their own perspectives on martyrdom.

As we have seen through this chapter debates about martyrdom appear in many different shapes and forms. In a digital age websites, blogs, photographs, posters, plays, murals, films, sermons, essays and speeches can swiftly become sites of contest. This is of course by no means restricted to the Middle East. In the remaining chapters, it will become even clearer that martyrdom is not only a contentious term, but also that debates about who is a martyr and what is a martyrdom can be found in many other diverse hitorical, cultural and religious contexts.

# Chapter 5
# **Reforming martyrdom**

In Europe during the mid 16th century, stories of contemporary and historic martyrdoms began to be widely circulated. This contributed to further debates about martyrdom. Following the invention and development of the printing press in the late 15th century, forms of communication had radically changed. Pamphlets, books, and pictures could be reproduced and circulated in just a few weeks, or even as little as several days. Printers and publishers became wealthy from their publications. While large books remained valuable objects, they were rarely transcribed by hand and no longer produced solely as luxury items to be owned by royalty, the nobility, and the church. At the same time Bibles, books, and pamphlets were increasingly published not only in Latin, but also in vernacular languages such as English, German, French, and Dutch. There is evidence that merchants, artisans, and other tradesmen purchased, read, and sold printed texts about martyrdoms both in Latin and in their own tongues. Even for those who could not read themselves, there were ever increasing numbers of printed books available that could be read from, and printed pictures to look at.

## Popularizing martyrdom

This expanding literary and visual culture combined with word of mouth to ensure that news about martyrdoms spread rapidly along trade routes and beyond. Such storytelling was a kind of religiously inspired journalism. Stories about recent violent events were news. They made for popular and dramatic copy. Particular deaths were given meaning and significance, which often then became bones of contention. Martyrdoms could be deeply divisive, especially as a number of public executions had taken place within living memory. In many cases they accentuated sectarian divides and became emotionally charged points of contest and debate. Once again martyrdom texts were not stable narratives, as they were re-described, re-formed, and recreated to serve the needs of both local and wider communities. Eyewitnesses, writers, and religious leaders wrote, collected, and edited detailed descriptions of gruesome deaths. These circulated around Europe, appearing from the 1550s in Dutch, French, German, and English martyrologies (literally, a list of martyrs). Compilers and editors appropriated other martyrdom stories, giving their own national histories of martyrdom an international flavour. In some cases these accounts informed the creation of printed pictures, mostly from woodcuts, which graphically illustrated individual martyrdoms.

Among the martyrologies of the 16th century *Foxe's Book of Martyrs* was the most popular and the best known, and arguably has had the most significant long-term impact on the understanding of martyrdom in the English-speaking world. The full title of the first edition, published in 1563, is *Actes and Monuments of these latter and perilous Dayes, touching matters of the Church, wherein are comprehended and described the great Persecution and horrible Troubles that have been wrought and practised by the Romishe Prelates*. In subsequent editions this title would change variously, though 'Book of Martyrs' was the popular title that would stick, even though Foxe was far from happy with this simplification, for he emphasized that his book contained 'many other matters'. Following the first English edition, which appeared in 1563, three further editions (1570, 1576, and 1583) were produced during John Foxe's lifetime (1517–87).

## Reforming martyrdom in historical context

King Henry VIII (1491–1547) bequeathed to his children a nation divided over religion. Henry had effectively made a declaration of independence from the pope's authority in 1534, when parliament legislated that he was 'supreme head' of the English church. As a result he was free to annul his marriage to Catherine of Aragon (1485–1536) and marry Anne Boleyn (d.1536). Henry may have dissolved the monasteries (1536–41) and been excommunicated by Pope Paul III (1538), but he remained largely loyal to Catholic beliefs.

Following Henry's death his 9-year-old son was crowned Edward VI (1537–53). Edward had been tutored in the ways of Protestantism. Under the direction of Archbishop Cranmer and several powerful nobles, the reformation from above accelerated during Edward VI's reign (1547–53). Reformers like John Foxe saw Edward as a 'godly prince' in the mould of King Josiah, who had brought about religious reform in Israel (2 Kings 22–23; 2 Chronicles 34–35). Foxe joined members of the Protestant elite, who supported the 'mass destruction' of Catholic rituals.

Following Edward's death his half-sister Mary (1516–58) took the reins of power (1553–8). A staunch Catholic, she initiated a radical turn back towards Catholicism. Hoping for a *rapprochement* with Rome, she was a driving force behind the persecution of reformers. Her opponents would come to call her 'Bloody Mary'. England swung back to Catholicism and Foxe feared for his life. He escaped with his pregnant wife and joined other exiles in Strasbourg. Here, and later in Basel, he was in a 'news hub' for receiving and recording reports of martyrdoms from around Europe. After Mary's death in 1558, and her half-sister Elizabeth's (1533–1603) accession to the throne, John Foxe, like other reformers, returned to his native land. What he had begun writing in Latin as an exile he now continued in English as a returnee. Foxe would find, in Queen Elizabeth's regime (1558–1603), fertile ground in which to sow his stories of martyrdom.

For each new edition Foxe incorporated fresh material, to include more recently received reports, to refute his Catholic critics, to correct mistakes, and to respond to the changed historical circumstances in which he wrote. The stories of martyrdom could be adapted and put to use in different contexts. It soon received official approval. In 1571 convocation ordered that the book be chained alongside the Bible in cathedral churches, an order that was extended to include some parish churches in England. The 1563 edition is an enormous book, larger even than many lectern Bibles: at about one foot long and 1,700 pages, it is impossible to lift comfortably with one hand. It proved extremely popular, so much so that the second expanded edition was rapidly published only seven years later, in 1570. This was made up of two volumes running to around 2,300 pages, containing over three million words. The number of illustrations also increased, more than doubling from 57 in the 1563 edition to 153 in the 1570 edition. The printer of the book, John Day, was a strong supporter of the project. He financed the woodcuts, which are often seen as one of the main reasons for *Foxe's Book of Martyrs'* huge popularity and considerable impact. In Books XI and XII they leave little to the imagination, showing martyrdom after martyrdom, often in graphic detail.

## Illustrating martyrdom

Why did *Foxe's Book of Martyrs* contain so many pictures? One aim appears to have been to attract a broad readership. Other reasons include to illustrate, to amplify, and to elaborate upon significant themes within the text. Persecution and martyrdom were brought to life. In some more expensive copies the black-and-white versions were even coloured to add greater realism to the events. In the 1570 edition a significant proportion of images (77 of the 153) cover the period of the persecutions of Mary (1553–8). Here is a form of Protestant iconography in which, a decade or two later, audiences could themselves become participants, watching with other members of the crowd. Many Protestants may have been deeply suspicious of the use of imagery for devotion, but this did not prevent them from using illustrations for 'edification'. Pictures enabled even those who could not read to ponder these spectacles.

The majority of the illustrations depict or are connected to scenes of death. Who needs to wonder what a martyrdom looked like when it is possible to see them in vivid line drawings? If you look at an original edition of the book, pages with the particularly graphic pictures are invariably more worn. There is evidence of drops of wax, food, or liquid on some of these illustrated pages. Some public houses owned copies, making the pictures available to a wider public, who might well have had a pint of ale in their hand as they enjoyed the illustrations. Clearly these images were magnets for readers and viewers. Some of the most dog-eared and stained pages portray the most famous burnings or most graphic scenes of violence. These include the woodcuts of the burning of Archbishop Thomas Cranmer in Oxford, Bishop Hooper in Gloucester, and perhaps most horrific of all a pregnant mother, Perotine Massey, in Guernsey (Book XI, 1570). In nearly four years of executions 284 people were burnt, 56 of whom were women. Perotine Massey was to be strangled and then burnt, but the 'rope brake' before she died and she tumbled into the fire. The 'vehemence of the flame' resulted in the baby boy bursting out of her 'belly' into the fire. At first he was fished out and laid on the grass nearby, but he was then thrown back into fire. The picture is entitled a 'Lamentable spectacle of three women . . .' and depicts the baby tumbling from the woman into the fire. The precise veracity of this 'Herodian crueltie' has been debated for several centuries. Many other pictures are more generic, representing martyrs engulfed in flames.

One of the best-known woodcuts from *Foxe's Book of Martyrs* depicts the moments immediately before the burning of Nicholas Ridley (1500–5) and Hugh Latimer (1487–1555) in Oxford on 16 October 1555 (Figure 8). Viewers are offered what several

**8. Hugh Latimer and Nicholas Ridley about to be burned, woodcut,**
*John Foxe's Book of Martyrs*, **1563 edition**

commentators describe as a 'bird's-eye view' of the action, as if
perched on a nearby tree and looking down over the execution of
these two 'degraded' bishops, like peering down into the crater of a
volcano. The artist has played with the perspective, tilting the
foreground down and background up in such a way as to show the
entire scene unobstructed. The visual heat of the crowd's gaze is
directed inwards, towards two bearded men, each tied by a single
iron chain to a stake. A man bends to pick up a faggot, presumably
to add it to the pyre, an upturned nest of wood that surrounds the
two bishops.

Latimer, the elder of the two and former bishop of Worcester, is
slightly hunched forward as a banderole (scroll) reveals some of
his final words, 'Father of Heaven receive my soul.' This recalls
Stephen's cry as he was stoned to death (Acts 7:59). Ridley,
formerly bishop of London, says in Latin, '*In man[us] tuas,
Domine*' ('Into thy hands, O Lord'). Foxe expands this in the text,

telling the reader that Ridley repeats this many times, adding
'I commend my spirit'. Ridley's prayer recalls Jesus' final words on
the cross, as recorded in the Gospel of Luke (23:46). English text
was used in the 1570 edition. Their words fly towards the crowd
and officials. They may be hemmed in up to their waists by
bundles of wood, but they boldly return the gaze of their
persecutors.

Unlike most of the illustrations of martyrdoms in Foxe's book, this
image captures the moments just before the main fire is actually
lit. In contrast to the woodcut of the execution of well-known
London preacher John Rogers, where the crowd appears up in
arms as he 'washes his hands in the flames' that engulf him, the
spectators here appear still, breathless, and expectant. The action
and contest have been compressed. To the right of the martyrs, in
a towering, sturdy portable pulpit, Dr Richard Smith preaches.
This is clear from the text within the picture, which includes an
abbreviated Latin verse from Paul's first letter to the church at
Corinth. ('I may give away all I possess, or even give my body to
be burnt, but if I have no love I gain nothing': 1 Corinthians 13:3).
Foxe describes this fifteen-minute address as a 'wicked sermon'.
By contrast, a bearded Cranmer, the imprisoned archbishop of
Canterbury, stands apart and above the wreath of people who
encircle the protagonists. He observes the execution from the
Bocardo prison tower and prays for his friends, 'O Lord
Strengthen them.' Through the preaching Smith and the praying
Cranmer, through the seated judges and the standing martyrs, this
picture captures two worlds colliding.

## Narrating martyrdom

While the images reinforce the graphic story of their deaths, Foxe's
written account provides agonizing detail of the actual burning of
Latimer and Ridley. He describes how Latimer dies swiftly and
apparently relatively painlessly. Not so Ridley. Foxe reveals that
the wood on the pyre is green and badly stacked, and this is made

worse by misjudged attempts to reposition the faggots. Rather than accelerating his death, this actually slows down the burning, and increases Ridley's agony. He cries out that he cannot burn. While the picture portrays them dignifiedly affirming their faith, the text provides more gory details of Ridley's suffering: his 'dreadful extremity was but too plain, for after his legs were quite consumed, he showed his body and shirt unsinged by the flame'. Only when he is able to lean into the flames and set off the gunpowder around his neck does he finally expire. The text and the image combine to encapsulate several themes found within Foxe's virulently anti-Catholic book: persecution, suffering, and martyrdom.

As in the illustration, the entire scene revolves around the two martyrs. The 1570 edition attributes to Latimer probably the most widely quoted (and often adapted) line from the entire book: 'Be of good comfort, Master Ridley; and play the man. We shall this day, by God's grace, lyght such a candle in England, as, I trust, shall never be put out.' This quotation resonates with Eusebius' description of Polycarp's 2nd-century martyrdom. As Polycarp enters the arena to face death, a 'voice from heaven' encourages him with the words: 'Be strong Polycarp and play the man.' Many scholars assume that as Latimer's words do not appear in the first 1563 edition, and by 1570 Foxe is writing fifteen years after their actual execution, he is embellishing this martyrdom. It is widely recognized that Foxe attempted to follow in the footsteps of Eusebius (see Chapter 2). Like Eusebius, Foxe is attempting to write a comprehensive history of the church, drawing on original or authoritative sources and concentrating on bearing witness through martyrdom. In this context it is as if Foxe has transformed Latimer and Ridley into Protestant saints, who are following in the footsteps of the founding martyrs of the early church. By providing a parallel between these martyrdom stories, Foxe underlines the continuity between the earliest Christians and these martyrs of the Reformation. Nevertheless, it is not beyond the bounds of possibility that the scholar Latimer also had such stories in his mind as he walked to his death. Making a connection between the early church and the Protestant communities was a common way of authenticating their own beliefs, both under the sympathetic reign of Edward VI and under the persecutions of Mary. Martyrdom stories were a way of highlighting the continuity between the practices of the 'pure' early church and the 'true' church of the 16th century. It was also a good way of answering the Catholic critics' question: where was the Protestant church before the Reformation?

Martyrdom stories were also used to show how persecutors are or will be punished. Some persecutors are portrayed as pantomime villains while others are more menacing. Several are demonized. There is Edmund Bonner (1500–69), bishop of London, who in several pictures is portrayed as sweaty and dirty, even beating a bare-bottomed 'heretic' himself in one picture. Later readers would even scratch out 'bloody Bonner's' eyes in one of the illustrations that depicts him torturing a prisoner. Foxe vilified him, using doggerel verse: 'This cannibal in three years space three hundred martyrs slew. They were his food, he loved so blood, he spared none he knew.' In another section Foxe describes how the bishop of Winchester, Stephen Gardiner (d.1555), did not live long enough to enjoy the news of his victories. According to Foxe, it was on the very day of Latimer and Ridley's execution that Gardiner, 'their great persecutor', was struck down with illness. He experienced 'great agonies' and 'excruciating pain which eventually put an end to his life'. Here is providential retribution for the persecutor. This is a recurring theme in both Protestant and Catholic martyrologies.

Alongside the punishments of the persecutors were placed the very real sufferings of the victims. Scenes such as the description of the death of John Hooper (d.1555), bishop of Gloucester and Worcester, do not spare the reader. In Book XI Foxe describes how Hooper's 'lippes went, till they were shrounke to the gommes: and he did knocke his brest with his hands until one of his armes fel of,

73

and then knocked still with the other, what time the fat, water, and bloud dropped out his fingers ends'. The illustration shows flames creeping up and around his body. He remains upright and dignified. A single woman in the crowd wipes a tear away from her eye. Foxe several times comments how bystanders wept or are moved to tears, implying that there was significant public outcry or support for the martyrs. Some historians have recently questioned the extent of public support provoked by the death of the likes of Hooper, Ridley, and Latimer. They suggest that Foxe was amplifying the grief and public outcry in order to diminish his ecclesial opponents and celebrate the value of the martyrdoms.

Another way of challenging the Catholic Church was through telling memorable stories of the heroic actions of Protestant martyrs. The story of the archbishop of Canterbury, Thomas Cranmer, stands out not simply because of his seniority, but also because of the dramatic nature of his trial, final recantation, and death. Cranmer had gone through six earlier recantations, and would have been more valuable to the Catholic cause alive and penitent than dead and martyred. Nevertheless, Mary appeared determined to punish Cranmer, who as archbishop had played a significant role in the divorce of her mother, Catherine of Aragon, from Henry VIII.

Just before his execution he was given a platform at the University Church of St Mary the Virgin in Oxford to recant one final time. He surprised everyone listening by going off-script:

> And now I come to the great thing which so much troubleth my conscience, more than any thing that ever I did or said in my whole life . . . which now here I renounce and refuse, as things written with my hand contrary to the truth which I thought in my heart, and written for fear of death, and to save my life, if it might be; and that is, all such bills or papers which I have written or signed with my hand since my degradation, wherein I have written many things untrue. And forasmuch as my hand hath offended, writing contrary

to my heart, therefore my hand shall first be punished; for when
I come to the fire it shall first be burned.

He proceeded to affirm Protestant views and denounce the pope
as 'Christ's enemy'. This 'unexpected declaration led to amazement
and indignation'. Foxe then connects Cranmer's action with
Samson, who brought 'a greater ruin upon his enemies in the hour
of death, than he did in his life'. This alludes to Judges 16:30 in the
Hebrew Bible, which tells of how the captive Samson's strength
returns which enables him to pull down the two central pillars of
the temple of Dagon, leading to its collapse on himself and also
'upon the rulers and all who are in it'. Cranmer would have
continued his speech, but he was dragged away under the cry of
'lead the heretic away'. He was taken to the same location, a ditch
close to Balliol College, where Latimer and Ridley had been burnt.
He then held his hand out 'unshrinkingly in the fire until it was
burnt to a cinder, even before his body was injured, frequently
exclaiming, "This unworthy right hand" . . . as long as his voice
would suffer him; and using often the words of Stephen, "Lord
Jesus, receive my spirit", in the greatness of the flame, he gave up
the ghost.' Once again the last words at the martyrdom are
highlighted. Foxe portrays several other martyrs as following in
the footsteps of Stephen, who was celebrated as the church's first
martyr.

Two pictures are used to illustrate this sequence of events. The
first shows Cranmer being dragged off a platform in the University
Church of St Mary's, while the other shows him bound in the fire
holding out his right hand into the flames. The focal point of the
picture is his index finger in the midst of the flames. While the
setting is the same as Latimer and Ridley's execution, the crowd is
closer to the martyr and more crushed as they look on. The series
of events surrounding Cranmer's death on 21 March 1556 is
commonly interpreted as a 'propaganda disaster' for the Marian
church. Foxe tells it with great relish, amplifying its significance.
The story of the Oxford martyrs (Latimer, Ridley, and especially

Cranmer) was widely disseminated. For example, there is evidence of a Latin version of Cranmer's martyrdom being read in Hungary in the mid-1560s. Today, in the middle of Broad Street in Oxford, a small cross of cobbled stones marks where they were executed. Nearby a Victorian Martyrs' Memorial (1840–2, Gilbert Scott) reminds passers-by how 'near this spot' Cranmer, Ridley, and Latimer 'yielded their bodies to be burned, bearing witness to the sacred truths which they had affirmed and maintained against the errors of the Church of Rome'. The creation of this memorial and this partisan inscription reflected Victorian anxiety about the growth of High Church Anglicanism. The Oxford martyrs' narrative continues to reverberate around the world. For instance, a 19th-century stained glass window commemorates their deaths for the 'principles of the Reformation' in an Episcopal church in Little Rock, Arkansas, USA.

Cranmer's death did trouble some contemporary viewers. For example, a letter written by one Catholic who witnessed the burning of Cranmer in Oxford reveals mixed emotions. He felt both admiration and sorrow, admiration for Cranmer's steadfastness and dignity as he died, but sadness that Cranmer had suffered for what he believed was the wrong cause. He wrestled with the question of what makes for a true martyrdom. His answer, commonly expressed in the 16th century, was that it is not the quality or reality of the death, but the cause of that death that makes for a true martyr (*non poena, sed causa*). This argument would be played out through narratives that challenged Foxe's entire project.

## Challenging martyrdoms

Martyrdoms can divide. Reactions to Foxe's book highlight this point. Critics swiftly denounced many of the words and images that celebrate martyrdom. Some questioned the accuracy and veracity of Foxe's accounts. Foxe himself was later contemptuously derided as a 'martyr-maker' or 'martyr-man'. One critic, a Catholic priest Thomas Harding (1516–72), wrote of that 'huge dunghill of your stinking martyrs' in 1565. The most sustained contemporary criticism appeared in 1566 and was written by Nicholas Harpsfield (1519–75), archdeacon of Canterbury under Queen Mary. Harpsfield produced a 1,000-page book (*Dialogi sex*) in which the last of the six dialogues was devoted to attacking Foxe's 1563 edition of *Acts and Monuments*. This took up over a quarter of the book and was easily the longest of Harpsfield's dialogues, running to over 250 pages. At the heart of his argument was the claim that those whom Foxe called martyrs could not be true martyrs because they had died not for the 'True Church' or for Christ, but rather for heretical beliefs. They were 'pseudomartyrs'. Their suffering and death could not transform them into true martyrs. Their fraudulence and Foxe's unreliability were further demonstrated by the fact that these 'pseudomartyrs' were described as insane or classed as criminals, suicides, drunkards, or demon-possessed.

One issue that provoked particular ire was an attempt to reorder the church year. At the start of the 1563 edition of *Foxe's Book of Martyrs* a controversial new calendar was inserted. What a Jesuit lay brother, Thomas Pounde (1539–1614), described in his 1582 poem as the the 'shufflinge' of saints 'from their invested dayes' stirred up considerable anger. Who was Foxe to appoint himself as judge of who was and who was not a saint or true martyr? According to Harpsfield, this was a 'monstrous inversion' as Foxe had tried to pull 'the true martyrs of Christ' down from heaven, while 'raising up Lucifer' to replace them. Harpsfield structured his own criticism of Foxe's book around this calendar. In this way he was able to contrast Foxe's 'heretics' with the 'true' historic martyrs. He went further, claiming that the early church martyrs were almost entirely educated clergy or theologians, or from the higher echelons of society, in contrast to the vast majority of Foxe's martyrs, who were poorly educated or from lowly backgrounds.

This claim was repeated, highlighted, and taken further by Robert Persons in his three-volume *A Treaties of Three Conversions of England from Paganism to Christian Religion* (1603–4). This can be read as a Catholic recasting of Foxe's *Acts and Monuments*. Even more methodically than Harpsfield before him, Persons lambasts the supposed replacement of the traditional Catholic calendar. In his second and third volumes he is deeply critical of Foxe's 'calendar-martyrs', who included weavers, cowherds, cobblers, tailors, and smiths. He contrasts these with 'our' 'true', learned, and 'saintly' martyrs. The 1563 calendar of martyrdoms and new saints may well have been included in the *Book of Martyrs* at the behest of the printer John Day. In the light of such criticisms it was transformed in later editions into something closer to an index at the back of the book.

Persons' criticisms went beyond the calendar. He expressed disdain for those, like Foxe, who 'bragged of martyrdom' but were in fact promoting not martyrs but murderers, thieves, and rebels as well as witches, sorcerers, and heretics. He objected to Foxe's representation of Cranmer as a true and constant martyr. For Persons, Cranmer was inconstant, prone to 'many turnings and wyndings'. Persons also had no time for the illustrations: he vigorously criticized the 'spectacle and representation of martyrdoms' which 'delighteth many to gaze on, who *cannot read*'. These were little more than a 'pleasant (or rather peevish) invention, to entertayne the eyes of the simple readers and *lookers on*, and to make pastime for fooles'.

Not only were the critics deconstructing *Foxe's Book of Martyrs*; they were also constructing contemporary Catholic martyrologies. Between 1566 and 1660 there were at least 50 works published relating to the persecution of Catholics in England. A good number of these texts described the deaths of the 239 English Catholics who were executed, mostly on charges of treason, between 1535 and 1603. These texts commonly affirmed their own claims that they died martyrs' deaths. The likes of Bishop John Fisher (1469–1535), Sir Thomas More (1478–1535), and the Jesuit Edmund Campion (1540–81) were portrayed as genuine martyrs of the 'true' church. Campion's torture and brutal execution by being hung, drawn, and quartered became one of a number of widely circulated Catholic martyrdom stories. These narratives also became subjects for artists. For instance, an 18th-century English engraving of Campion includes his torture on the rack and his execution at Tyburn in the background.

This counter-visual history of martyrdom had been developed earlier. For example, a book of engravings, *Ecclesiae Anglicanae Trophaea*, was published in 1584, which included graphic 'martyr murals' from the English College chapel in Rome. These frescoes, by Niccoló Circignani, portrayed both past and present English martyrs. During the Catholic or Counter-Reformation in the late sixteenth and early seventeenth centuries artists returned to depicting martyrdom, a topic that had been popular during the Middle Ages. For example, in his portrait of *St Catherine of Alexandria* (*c*.1598) Caravaggio painted a well-known courtesan (Fillide Melandroni) as the probably legendary 4th-century martyr Catherine of Alexandria, wearing a purple robe, kneeling on a red cushion, with a martyr's palm by her feet (Figure 9). Caravaggio portrays Catherine holding a sword and leaning, almost nestling, towards a spiked wheel. According to tradition the wheel shattered when she touched it, so she was instead beheaded.

Not all portrayals of martyrdom are so seductive. The Anglo-Dutch Richard Verstegan's book, *Theatrum Crudelitatum* (1583, revised *c*.1604) included alongside its gruesome tales of torture, cruelty, and Catholic martyrdoms in Europe, a number of explicit images, several of which were probably drawn by the author himself. The book includes a picture of Margaret Clitherow (1556–86), the 30-year-old mother of four being pressed to death in York on Good Friday 1586. This butcher's wife had hosted Masses in the attic of her house in the Shambles, York. Convicted of harbouring priests, she refused to testify, in order to try to save her children from being interrogated and tortured. The result was that she was executed by being pressed to death, effectively having her back broken. Some see the retelling of Clitherow's martyrdom as a counter-martyrdom story to tales about Anne Askew (1520/1–46),

9. Michelangelo Merisi da Caravaggio, *Saint Catherine of Alexandria*, oil on canvas, *c.*1598

who had been tortured and executed for denying one of the central Catholic doctrines, transubstantiation. Nonetheless, the majority of celebrated Catholic martyrs tended to be educated clergy and male, and therefore easy to distinguish from what is sometimes described as 'the unlearned riff-raff thronging the pages of Foxe'. Many of these martyrdom stories were employed not simply to win theological arguments but also to galvanize support in mainland Europe for a Spanish invasion to oust Elizabeth and her Protestant government, thereby reconquering England for the 'true faith'.

Challenges to Foxe have continued over the last four centuries. The lasting significance of Foxe's work can be seen by the fact that even 250 years after its publication it was still attracting detailed criticism. Best known is William Eusebius Andrews' *A Critical and Historical Review of Foxe's Book of Martyrs: Shewing the Inaccuracies, Falsehoods, and Misrepresentations in that Work of Deception* (1824). In this book 'the pseudo-martyrs of Fox's Church' are once again contrasted with 'the Missionary Catholic Priests who suffered death under Protestant Laws'. The controversy over who controlled the histories of martyrdom continued for several hundred years in Europe.

## Evolving martyrdoms

*Foxe's Book of Martyrs* was a text that could be adapted, expanded, and developed. It was more malleable than the Bible. Initially Foxe played a vital role in the evolving narrative. For example, he included in the fourth edition of 1583 a brief 'reminder' of the St Bartholomew's Day Massacre (August 1572), where several thousand Protestants were killed in Paris, and then in several other cities in France. Even after Foxe's death in 1587 the *Book of Martyrs* continued to evolve, addressing contemporary events such as the attempted invasion by the Spanish Armada in 1588 and the Gunpowder Plot of 1605. These martyrdom stories became particularly popular among Puritans and Low Country Protestants in the 17th century. By 1684 nine complete editions had been published. This process of reproduction and expansion continued not only through the seventeenth but also the eighteenth and nineteenth centuries, with new versions and adaptations published at regular intervals. These included publications such as Edward Bulkley's *The Book of Martyrs* (1732) and Henry Southwell's *The New Book of Martyrs* (1764–5). There are many other derivative 'Books of Martyrs', which are sometimes described as 'continuing Foxe'.

These books about martyrdom have been put to different uses at different times. There appears to have been increased interest in *Foxe's Book of Martyrs* following the French Revolution in 1789 and the European revolutions of 1848. What did these martyrdom stories have to say in the face of the public promotion of atheism in France? Following the deaths of many Catholics during the revolution, might any of them be classed as new martyrs? For those working for Catholic emancipation between the 1770s and 1820s Foxe's book was perceived as an obstacle to making Catholicism more legally acceptable in Britain. Others drew upon the martyrdom stories as a way of trying to incite anti-Catholic feeling and thereby block this movement, which culminated in the 1829 Catholic Relief Act. Different groups used different versions of the book to promote particular viewpoints. This can be seen in the publication and uses of adapted versions such as John Milner's *Universal History of Christian Martyrdom* (1807) and Henry More's *History of the Persecutions* (1810). One editor, Stephen Reed Cattley, even produced a huge eight-volume edition under the title *The Acts and Monuments of John Foxe: A New and Complete Edition* (1837). This version was largely sponsored by the Evangelicals or Low Church Anglicans who were anxious about the increasing dominance of Anglo-Catholics through the Oxford Movement. There is a sense, however, in which this book was never completed in that it was continually added to over several hundred years. With the digitization of the entire text in the 21st century, it has taken on a new existence and is far more accessible.

Alongside the expanded editions, abridged versions became increasingly popular. The first abridged edition, compiled by Timothy Bright, appeared in 1589, only two years after Foxe's death.

Clement Cotton's 240-page *The Mirror of Martyrs* (1613) was much more affordable, and went through at least nine editions between 1613 and 1685. Abridgement, abbreviation, and selection would continue for the next four centuries. Among these significantly shortened versions, the second volume and last two books of the 1570 version were particularly popular. These abridged versions were often largely made up of the Marian martyrdoms. The papers, letters, and documents, as well as the connections with Eusebius and the early church were often abbreviated or even entirely cut out, thereby radically changing the overall meaning of the book. The result was that the book evolved into a 'Book of Martyrs' that was invariably dominated by a series of violent martyrdom stories. The founding father of Methodism, John Wesley, for example, condensed the stories of martyrs, edited out references to the pope, and largely removed the secular history. In the 19th century there were small editions of Foxe's work sold by the Birmingham Protestant Association which measured little more than three inches and were ideal for the pocket, including one for a penny. Even earlier, in 1616, a tiny matchbox-sized version had been produced. Foxe's text appears also to have influenced the creation of poetry and ballads and the preservation of local martyrdom stories throughout Britain.

More significantly, some believe that these stories contributed less to the formation of a lasting national church and more to an image of what being British meant. From this perspective, these martyrdom tales helped to define British, or perhaps English, identity. In short this identity was 'not Catholic'. Abridged, derivative, and expanded versions underlined how it was Catholics who had persecuted the preachers of the truth, cruelly killed godly martyrs in Mary's reign, planned the destruction of parliament, and killed many Protestants during the Irish Rebellion of 1641. These martyrdom stories arguably contributed to a visceral fear of 'Continental popery'. Several of these new editions underlined how Catholics were alien, different, and not to be trusted. For some 'the smoke of the fires of Smithfield', representing many Protestant martyrdoms, 'got in all our eyes', and heightened anti-Catholic sentiment in Britain. The extent to which these martyrdom stories shaped national identity and divisions remains a live discussion.

Foxe's work, and other martyrologies, had an international impact. Almost a hundred years after *Foxe's Book of Martyrs* appeared, Thieleman J. van Braght produced a 1,290-page book in Dutch entitled *Martyrs' Mirror* (1660). Its full title was *The Bloody Theater; or Martyrs' Mirror of the Defenseless Christians who baptized only upon confession of faith, and who suffered and died for the testimony of Jesus their Saviour, from the time of Christ to the year A.D. 1660*. Van Braght drew on a number of Foxe's accounts, as well as on local Dutch, German, and Swiss sources. This huge and detailed collection, which includes a significant number of Anabaptist martyr and martyrdom stories, was reprinted several times and was later translated into German (1748–9) and into English in the USA (1837). One element that distinguishes this book from Foxe's is the word 'defenceless', which refers to the belief that the Anabaptists neither resisted their persecutors nor used violence to promote their beliefs.

One of the most famous stories from the *Martyrs' Mirror* is of Dirk Willems's capture and execution near his hometown of Asperen in the Netherlands. He was being

> hotly pursued by a thief-catcher, and as there had been some frost, said Dirk Willems ran before over the ice, getting across with considerable peril. The thief-catcher following him broke through, when Dirk Willems, perceiving that the former was in danger of his life, quickly returned and aided him in getting out, and thus saved his life. The thief-catcher wanted to let him go, but the burgomaster very sternly called to him to consider his oath, and thus he was again seized by the thief-catcher, and, at said place, after severe

imprisonment and great trials proceeding from the deceitful
papists, put to death at a lingering fire.

The author goes on to make clear that even though the east wind
blew away the fire, resulting in a slow death, Willems remained
'steadfast'. Probably the best-known image, out of 104 represented
in the 1685 edition, is Jan Luiken's (1649–1712) illustration
depicting Willems rescuing one of his pursuers from falling
through the ice (Figure 10). This picture, showing not Willems's
martyrdom but an act of charity towards his enemies, was
commonly found in Mennonite and other Anabaptist homes.

Images of martyrdom are put to different uses in various cultural
and historical contexts. Martyrdom is constantly being re-formed.
There are a number of striking similarities between Protestant
and Catholic representations of martyrdom. Both celebrate

10. Jan Luiken, *Dirk Willems Saves his Pursuer*, etching, *Martyrs'
Mirror*, 1685 edition

exemplary lives and deaths, contrasted with the persecutor's villainy. Both emphasize the virtues of resolve, steadfastness, and sacrifice. Both compete for dominance of the symbolic language that circulates around martyrdoms. Being burnt or tortured to death was agonizing, shameful, and ignoble. So the narratives and illustrations in both Catholic and Protestant books attempt to dignify the victim. Both tend to emphasize the pious last words of the martyr, even drawing on the traditions of *ars moriendi* (the 'art of dying'), the noble death, or voluntary violent death. Even the martyrs themselves play their own roles in rituals of death and regaining dignity, kissing the stake, raising their hands in prayer or giving away their last worldly possessions just before they are killed. Wearing white, thin robes may have speeded up death, but they also recalled the white-robed army of martyrs found in the book of Revelation.

# Chapter 6
# Politicizing martyrdom

Leaders who are killed sometimes exert more influence dead than alive. Rulers who might largely have been forgotten are sometimes particularly remembered because of how or why they died. The Danish philosopher-theologian Søren Kierkegaard (1813–55) famously claimed in his journals that 'The tyrant dies and his rule is over; the martyr dies and his rule begins' (1848). The power of a martyr is hard to predict, but it can live on beyond the grave. A martyr's actual life may be comparatively short, but their 'rule' as a martyr may last many centuries after their demise. As we have seen, certain deaths are invested with more significance than others. Some martyrdoms are like passing comets, shining faintly as they flash across the firmament. With a few exceptions, these deaths attract either brief interest or pass by largely unnoticed and are ultimately forgotten. If their memory is preserved and circulated, however, then they can remain in view like brightly shining stars, their story travelling across time and space to subsequent generations.

## Preserving martyrdoms

Arguably the most significant thing that several monarchs did was to die in such a way as to allow their deaths to be described as martyrdoms and themselves as martyrs. Who murdered the English King Edward (c.962–78) near Corfe Castle in Dorset is debated; so too is why he was killed. One early source describes how he was murdered as he dismounted. Victorian portrayals show him drinking mead on his horse as he is about to be fatally stabbed. It is possible that his stepmother, Queen Elfrida (945–1000), wishing her own son to be king, instigated his murder. Nevertheless, within a few years his death was being remembered as a martyrdom, and he was being called Edward the Martyr. Historians debate why a cult developed commemorating his death. While some see this as a grass-roots popular movement, others believe that Edward's former followers used his death as a way to challenge the new king, his half-brother Æthelred (c.968–1016). It is also possible that Æthelred and his supporters used memories of Edward as a martyr and saint to bolster his own regime, as they attempted to galvanize the population to fight the Danes. Stories were later circulated that the popular reforming Archbishop Dunstan (c.909–88) sternly warned the new king at his coronation of the dangers of coming to power through Edward's death. In short, different groups may well have used Edward's death and martyrdom in different ways to serve their own political and religious ends. It appears that Æthelred enabled the creation of a shrine for Edward's remains to be preserved at Shaftesbury Abbey in 1001. This became a popular place of pilgrimage, attracting pilgrims from all over the country and beyond. Alphege (c.954–1012), Dunstan's successor as the Archbishop of Canterbury, who was himself to be martyred by the Vikings, canonized Edward in 1008. The roughly contemporaneous Anglo-Saxon Chronicle claimed that 'men murdered' Edward 'but God has magnified him; in life he was an earthly king, but after death he is now a heavenly saint'.

His martyrdom continued to be commemorated as such in the 19th century. For example, a Victorian edition of *Foxe's Book of Martyrs* includes a line drawing of Edward on a white horse, drinking from a goblet, while a man approaches him from behind, knife poised, to stab him in the back. A sinister-looking woman, presumably his stepmother, looks on. This scene was reproduced in a number of 19th-century illustrations, reflecting a fascination with this story of familial betrayal and royal martyrdom. The 20th century saw a further development of his cult. His remains were rediscovered in a casket in the 1930s, having supposedly been hidden during the dissolution of the monasteries under King Henry VIII in the 16th century. In the early 1970s it was claimed by a professional osteologist that these were Edward's actual bones. Having studied them carefully, he asserted at the end of a lengthy report: 'I cannot escape the conviction on historical, anatomical and surgical grounds that, beyond all reasonable doubt, we have here the bones of St Edward, King and Martyr.' This assertion was used by various groups as 'proof' that a physical connection existed with a medieval martyr. After some dispute these remains were given to the Russian Orthodox Church Outside of Russia to preserve. They have established a shrine at St Edward the Martyr Church in Brookwood, Surrey, alongside a small residence for the brotherhood of St Edward the Martyr Orthodox monks. They commissioned a contemporary artist to paint an icon of St Edward the Martyr. In this modern icon he holds a cross and a sword and his attire is reminiscent of older depictions of Byzantine saints. The monks and the wider Orthodox Church Outside of Russia describe Edward as a 'passion-bearer', someone who faced his death with resignation, not necessarily for his beliefs, but in a manner similar to Christ.

## Depicting Russian martyrdoms

While the St Edward the Martyr Orthodox Brotherhood's website provides extensive details about Edward the Martyr, it makes clear that he is by no means the only royal or Orthodox martyr to be remembered. His apparent death and transformation from victim to saint and martyr is paralleled with another more famous royal martyrdom: that of Tsar Nicholas II and his family in 1918. They were killed, along with several of their closest servants, in the early hours of 17 July 1918 by the Bolsheviks in the basement of Ipatiev

House in Yekaterinburg, Russia. It is claimed by one eyewitness that Nicholas's last words echoed Jesus' on the cross: 'You know not what you do.' The location of their execution is now marked by the Church on Blood. In 2000 the Moscow Synod of the Russian Orthodox Church described Nicholas II and his wife, Alexandra, and their five children Olga, Tatiana, Maria, Anastasia, and Alexis not only as 'saints' but also as 'passion-bearers', who bore their suffering 'with humility, patience, and meekness'. There are some within the Orthodox Church who believe that they cannot be classed as 'martyrs' because they did not die for their religious faith, but for political reasons (the Bolsheviks were concerned that the White Army might liberate them and they would become a focal point for resistance). This debate remains live. Even though they are not formally known as martyrs, they are commonly referred to in popular publications, icons, and devotions in these terms.

The Russian Orthodox Church Abroad went a step further by canonizing them in 1981 as 'new martyrs', along with their doctor, cook, maid, and footman, who had been killed at the same time. Their status as martyrs can be seen represented in many contemporary icons. In several churches in both St Petersburg and Moscow it is possible to find icons depicting the royal family. This is also true of icons in Orthodox churches outside Russia. Consider the icon of *The New Martyrs of Russia who Suffered Death for Christ* (1981), painted for the Holy Epiphany Church in Boston, by the iconographer N. A. Papkov (1906–94) (Figure 11). This is a highly charged political representation of martyrdom, though at first sight it is easy to interpret it purely as a devotional object. At the centre of this 3 by 4 foot icon are over fifty haloed figures in ordered rows. There is a clear sense of hierarchy in this icon of martyrs. At the front are some of the 'royal passion-bearers'. In the centre of the first row is the teenage Tsarevich Alexis wearing a red cloak. Some contemporary Orthodox writers regard him as particularly significant because he was the crown prince. 'Alexis was destined for martyrdom from the moment of his birth: the

**11. N. A. Papkov, *The New Martyrs of Russia who Suffered Death for Christ*. The original icon was painted for the Holy Epiphany Church in Boston, Massachusetts, USA, in 1981**

only and beloved son, he was the young Isaac who was actually sacrificed, the innocent sacrificial lamb who was worthy to atone for the sins of his people.' In the icon Alexis' parents are directly behind him. His father, the tsar, has his hand on his shoulder, while his mother stands behind him holding a cross in her hand. Their daughters surround them, dressed as nurses or Russian Sisters of Mercy, the role they took on during the First World War.

This group is surrounded by a number of senior Orthodox clergy who were killed soon after the 1917 revolutions. They are often described as *hieromartyrs* and include Patriarch Tikhon and four Metropolitans. Beyond them are largely anonymous figures, including priests, monks, and children. It is not possible to make out all the faces, giving the impression of an endless number of martyrs. Their sanctity is highlighted by at least six angels in the background, twelve crowns (of victory) descending from heaven, and the fact that one of the new martyrs is holding an icon of Mary (who is known within the Orthodox tradition as *Theotokos*, Mother of God). The white church behind the Orthodox cross is reminiscent of the Church on Blood in Yekaterinburg. The vast majority of the viewers face the viewer of the icon. There is very little blood and no explicit sign of suffering. The cumulative impact of this central panel is to show martyrs glorified, dignified, and at peace.

This central panel stands in sharp contrast to fourteen separate narrative panels that surround the main picture. Encircling a central image with smaller pictures is a common approach in icon painting. These reveal a series of brutal deaths, described as martyrdoms. They begin in the top left corner with what a later commentary on the icon describes as the 'murder of the Royal family'. Several bodies litter the floor. A light-haired boy (Alexis) crumples while a single girl in white cringes away from the bullets. Her arm points upwards. On the wall above the bodies, blood has been used to scrawl occult-like symbols. Some claim that the martyrdom of the royal family was followed by 'the martyrdom of millions of Orthodox Christians'. It is hard to be precise about exact numbers, but it is clear that during several waves of persecution many thousands of clergy and lay people were killed for their religious beliefs.

It is easier to remember specific individuals than thousands of faceless martyrs. This icon brings the persecutions to life by portraying specific martyrdoms. On the top right, Metropolitan Vladimir is depicted kneeling in front of the gates of the Kiev Caves monastery, where he was killed in early 1918. He is surrounded by several figures with bayonets, while another raises his sword as if to strike. Beneath him another metropolitan, Benjamin of St Petersburg, stands in front of trees, facing a firing squad. Following a trial in which he was 'convicted' of confiscating church treasures, he was executed, with three other clergy, in 1922. It is believed that they were dressed in rags and shaved, so the soldiers would not know that they were killing clergymen. One account later described how 'Metropolitan Benjamin went to his death calmly, whispering a prayer and crossing himself'. Beneath him is a prostrate figure engulfed in flames. Unlike many of the faces depicted in *Foxe's Book of Martyrs*, the face in this icon is hard to make out. This burning in the Far East of an Orthodox priest, Joachim Frolov, acts as a reminder of the other prisoners who suffered a similar fate in the early years of the Bolshevik regime.

The bottom three pictures illustrate life in the gulags. These were the camps which were run by the Chief Administration of Corrective Labour Camps and Colonies, better known as GULAG. These three images reflect the belief that these harsh and brutal camps became sites of martyrdom. The picture in the bottom right corner shows two guards beating, or 're-educating', a prisoner, while in the background prisoners line up in the snow waiting for their food. In the next rectangular picture, guards stand alongside a crowd of prisoners disembarking from cattle trucks. A priest in black with a pectoral cross and white beard walks close to the guard's dog. It is hard not to think of other pictures from the 20th century of lines of bedraggled prisoners lining up near cattle trucks. This is even more the case with the final image of two men hauling a skeletal corpse towards a pit. Here, according to one Orthodox interpreter, is a 'Russian Golgotha'.

The pictures on the left-hand side depict further martyrdoms, alongside other political critiques. In several the symbols of Christianity have been replaced by the symbols of communism. Not all Orthodox leaders necessarily accepted judgement, persecution, and death as passively as many of the figures in this icon appear to have done. In an appeal 'To the Orthodox People' the patriarch of Moscow, Tikhon (1865–1925), suggested during the Russian Civil War (1917–23) that the Soviet government should be resisted and that 'It is better to shed one's blood and to be awarded the martyr's crown than to let the enemies desecrate the Orthodox faith'.

These and other icons depicting new martyrs are put to a range of religious and political uses. Interpretation of this image can be significantly enriched not only by carefully scrutinizing each individual image, but also by studying a commentary on this icon taken from a North American website dedicated to 'New Martyrs for Christ', which is now to be found on the 'Our Faith' section of the 2012 website of an Orthodox parish in Virginia, All Saints in North America. This detailed commentary draws from a series of articles on 'New Martyrs' published in 1981 in the journal *Orthodox America*. Such articles and websites are part of a movement to preserve and publicize the many martyrdoms in Russia during the 20th century. The royal martyrdoms are the tip of an iceberg. Like the royal martyrs or passion-bearers controversy, debates continue over other individual cases. Some even write of 'false martyrs', reminiscent of the term used in 16th- and 17th-century Europe, 'pseudo-martyrs'. Who is and who is not a martyr has pertinence for contemporary church politics.

Even more significant is the era when these interpretations and representations were produced. Consider how the icon of *The New Martyrs of Russia who Suffered Death for Christ* was created in 1981, at a time when the communist government continued to exert control over Orthodoxy and other religious traditions in Russia. The apparent power of the communist government to persecute is made clear in many of the side panels. The central image, however, trumps all these 'minor' images. While the suffering is not diminished, the power in this icon resides in the central picture full of the 'glorified'. Such images are attempting to wrest back control of history. The martyrdoms are portrayed not as being the end of the story but as a moment in a movement towards glory. Identity is defined not by a national flag—the sickle and star of communism—but rather by a community of martyrs who are now part of a heavenly host bearing witness to different foundations of the nation and different leaders for building a civil society. While this icon, like its interpreters, is politically charged, its force does not derive from a political manifesto but rather from a vision of the world inspired by religious belief. It is common to find within Orthodox liturgies prayers such as: 'O Holy New martyrs and Confessors of the Russian land, by thy Holy prayers intercede for us.' From this outlook the martyrs in heaven take on a role of praying for those on earth. Even after the fall of communism a 21st-century Orthodox religious community in North America, who are not themselves being violently persecuted, have appropriated a thirty-year-old icon to highlight martyrdom as one of the defining characteristics of their own identity.

## Royal martyrdoms

What happens to the collective identity of an entire nation if its 'head' is literally cut off? In ways not dissimilar to the reactions towards Edward's and Nicholas's deaths, there was a wide range of responses to the beheading for 'high treason' of Charles I (1600–49) outside the Banqueting House in London on 30 January 1649. One particularly striking response was the development of the cult of King Charles the Martyr following his execution. His reported final words on the scaffold may not have been heard by many of the assembled crowds, but they would soon be printed and widely circulated. Sermons and pamphlets were later constructed around Charles's final statements. They reflect a calm and dignified state of mind: 'I have forgiven all the world, and even those in particular that have been the chief causers of my death.' Given the violent divisions in England through the Civil Wars, his final assertions were politically charged. He claimed that he had acted 'For the people; And truly I desire their liberty and freedom as much as anybody whomsoever'. The implication is clear that he was dying not for himself but for the 'liberty and freedom' of the people. For Charles and many of his followers, 'a subject and a sovereign are clean different things', and only if the nation was ordered in this way would they 'enjoy themselves'. He is reported to have gone on to say: 'I am the martyr of the people. I have a good cause and a gracious God on my side…I go from a corruptible, to an incorruptible Crown; where no disturbance can be, no disturbance in the World.' Some people were horrified when they heard the news of this regicide. Some fasted, some lamented, and others prayed. Stories circulated that a handkerchief with his blood had healed a blind girl. All this contributed to the establishment of the cult of Charles the Martyr.

It was, however, the publication of *Eikon Basilike* (Royal Portrait) in February 1649, less than two weeks after his death, that helped to establish the memory of Charles as a suffering king who was following in the footsteps of his own martyred Lord. The full title, *Eikon Basilike: The Pourtraiture of His Sacred Majestie in His Solitudes and Sufferings*, poignantly underlines the isolation and hardships faced by the monarch. This short book appears to provide a window to Charles's innermost thoughts as he prepares for his death. It is written in a simple and accessible style, justifying Charles's political actions during the Civil Wars, while also forgiving those behind his execution. Here is an innocent victim facing his death with courage. Some believe that the book was partly ghost-written by his chaplains, others that it emerged from a number of different writers. Precisely who wrote or edited the book is much debated, but it proved extremely popular, thirty-six editions being published within a year of Charles's death. It appears to have been read more widely than the radical Levellers' tracts (such as the series of manifestos entitled *An*

*Agreement of the People* 1647–9), which demanded more egalitarian forms of government, legal equality, and greater religious tolerance.

The frontispiece (the engraving on the book's first page) to *Eikon Basilike* was used so often that the engraver, William Marshall (active *c*.1617–49), had to replace the plate at least seven times (Figure 12). What does it depict? It shows the king kneeling in a chapel. His face is agonized, reminiscent of portrayals of Christ in the garden of Gethsemane, as he prays for the cup of suffering to be taken from him. His crown of the realm lies at his feet. Above the discarded crown of England is written '*Splendidam & Gravem*' (Splendid and Heavy). It is possible to make out, inscribed on its rim, '*vanitas*' (vanity). It is clear that Charles has

12. William Marshall (d. *c*.1649), engraving, frontispiece to *Eikon Basilike*, 1649

rejected this earthly crown. Instead, he grasps a crown of thorns with his right hand. In the middle of these intermeshed thorns is printed '*gratia*' (grace). Above this sharp crown, on a banderole, are the words '*Asperam & Levem*' (Bitter and Light). He gazes upwards at a vision of the heavenly crown, on which is inscribed beneath five stars '*gloria*' (glory). This allegorical engraving was commonly accompanied by explanatory sentences. The first edition had several verses, including these phrases attributed to the king:

> That Splendid, but yet toilsom Crown
> Regardlessly I trample down.
> With joie I take this Crown of thorn
> Though sharp, yet easie to be born.
> That heavn'nlie Crown, already mine
> I view with eies of Faith diuine.

Consider how these verses resonate with the picture, as one crown is replaced with another. Though the earthly crown remains 'splendid', this poem promotes a new way of looking at earthly power. The engraving, like the *Eikon Basilike* itself, uses religious symbols and metaphors to make political points. It is hard to disentangle the religious from the political motivations and uses of this book.

Nevertheless, many scholars believe that the dignity with which Charles carried himself at his death, his self-description as a 'martyr', and the cult which arose promoting his martyrdom contributed to royalism continuing as a viable alternative, standing in the wings in case the republic under Cromwell failed. Moreover the seeds of this approach were sown before his death, with Royalist writers and preachers portraying Charles in saintly terms during his captivity. Both Anglicanism and Royalism would go into exile: by preserving and elaborating upon Charles's dignified 'sacrifice' they were able to represent his death as a holy martyrdom on behalf of the people, the church, and the nation. On the restoration of his son Charles II to the throne, what had been informally practised became formalized in the Book of

Common Prayer, with a day of fasting, repentance, and commemoration of Charles to be held every year on 30 January. In 1660 the convocations of Canterbury and York canonized King Charles. While this day was removed from the calendar in 1859, the Society of King Charles the Martyr (originally established as a 'Church Defence Union under the banner of the Martyr-King') was founded in 1894 not only to promote veneration of King Charles but also to pray for the 'defence of the Church of England against the attacks of her enemies' and to campaign to reinstate Charles's commemoration day in the Church of England's calendar. The Royal Martyr Church Union, established in 1906, has similar aims.

In much the same way as several English churches were named after 'St Edward—king and martyr', so churches were named after 'St Charles—king and martyr'. After his death Charles's image as a saintly martyr was both more stable, in that he was no longer alive to corrupt it, and more malleable, in that followers could use it to their own ends without correction. It was not until the 'glorious revolution' of 1688, when the Protestant William and Mary replaced the Catholic James II on the throne, and the death of the last Stuart monarch, Queen Anne, in 1714 that the cult began to fragment into different political and theological outlooks.

The 18th century saw the French Revolution begin in 1789 and Louis XVI (1754–93) beheaded by the guillotine on 21 January 1793. It appears to have been less dignified than the beheading of Charles I, with some misunderstandings on the scaffold over how he was to be restrained. His final words are preserved as: 'I die as an innocent, for I'm innocent of the crimes of which I'm accused. I tell you this from the scaffold; I'm ready to stand before God. I forgive all those responsible for my death.' The drums drowned out any remaining words that Louis spoke. On 1 February 1793, a few days after his execution, the British artist Isaac Cruickshank produced an engraving entitled *The Martyrdom of Louis XVI, King of France*. Louis is depicted alone on the scaffold. Next to him is the guillotine. Through dark clouds, shafts of light shine upon the king. This print portrays Louis like an actor delivering a soliloquy with little more than a flag, a couple of bugles, and a wall of bayonets in the background as his audience. He is a tragic figure not only to be viewed and 'gently mocked', but also to be pitied. This anti-revolutionary print reflects how swiftly his death was described as a 'martyrdom'. It also reveals a change of mood towards the turmoil in France. Popular opinion in Britain appears to have largely swung against the revolution following Louis's execution, partly because of the memories that it evoked of Charles's execution, another regicide, and the turmoil that had followed in Britain during the previous century.

In 1793, a few months after Louis's death, a requiem mass and memorial services were held in his honour in Italy. Louis's surviving daughter, Marie-Thérèse Charlotte, vigorously lobbied in Rome for her father to be canonized as a saint. Four years after his death Pope Pius VI described Louis as 'a martyr'. This was not enough, however, for him to be canonized, as the Rome-based Catholic Congregation of Rites published a memorandum underlining that it was impossible to prove conclusively whether Louis was executed for religious or for political reasons. Nevertheless, it is still possible to attend worship services or to read accounts in which he is described as a martyr both in France and beyond. His son, commonly known even if not crowned as Louis XVII (1785–95), attracted considerable attention. Stories emerged that he had escaped, as similar rumours had with Tsar Nicholas II's son, Alexis. Others celebrated him as a *petit roi martyr*. It is clear from the discovery of remains and DNA testing that Louis XVII died in captivity and Alexis died in the basement with the rest of his family. These recent discoveries have reinforced claims that both actually died and perished as martyrs.

## Protesting martyrdoms

Up to this point in the chapter we have largely concentrated on how monarchs have been celebrated as martyrs. Some, like Charles II, appear to have embraced martyrdom, while others, like Nicholas II, appear to have been surprised by its suddenness. A further example illustrates not how a monarch was brought low but rather how a woman was killed by the king's horse in England. On 4 June 1913 the suffragette Emily Davison (1872–1913) travelled by train, with a return ticket, to Epsom. She had also purchased a ticket for a suffragette dance in the evening. On these grounds some historians claim that she was not seeking martyrdom. Others believe that her dramatic actions speak louder than her ticket purchases. She joined several thousand spectators, including the king and queen, to watch the English Derby. Pathé News was filming the race, and caught Davison's next actions in black-and-white. The short sequence is now easily accessible, reproduced several times on websites such as YouTube. It is hard to make out, as it happens so swiftly, but it appears that Davison waits and then steps out in front of the king's horse, Anmer, as it rounds Tattenham Corner. She is knocked down. Her hat tumbles across the racetrack. A witness recalls that she was carrying a WPSU (Woman's Social and Political Union) banner. Even though the horse also fell briefly to the ground, and the rider (Herbert Jones) was concussed, both would recover swiftly. Davison, however, who was hit in the head by the horse's hooves, died four days later from her injuries. The event was caught on film, ensuring that her death is firmly lodged in the collective memory of the suffragette struggles.

Davison's action provoked mixed responses. Many newspapers ran deeply critical reports and editorials, describing her actions on Derby Day as fanatical and 'reckless', interpreting them as 'unbalanced', 'demented', and 'desperately wicked'. By contrast she was celebrated by the WSPU as a 'martyr'. While this was a political protest, some suffragettes would interpret her actions in

**13. Cover of *The Suffragette*, 13 June 1913**

religious terms. In speeches and publications supporters would even connect her and other suffragettes' sufferings with the sufferings of the early Christians. On 27 June 1913, nearly three weeks after her death, *The Suffragette* published the simple headline 'A Christian Martyr'. On the front cover of this special memorial edition of the paper is an angelic-looking picture of Davison on the racetrack in front of the railings (Figure 13). She now has wings and a halo. (An article in the paper also underlines how the suffragettes' patron saint is Joan of Arc.) Notice how the significance of a political protest is accentuated by its connection with religious themes and symbols. Their respect for the monarchy and incredulity at what she had done led some to suggest that Davison's death hampered the suffragette cause. Far more beneficial to the cause were the so-called 'daily martyrdoms' of women as workers during the First World War. Nevertheless, Davison's funeral was widely publicized and the memory of her 'martyrdom on the racetrack' was often used to make political points by the suffragette movement.

## Founding martyrdoms

The execution of a Filipino writer, poet, sculptor, and ophthalmologist by the name of José Rizal in Manila, at 7.03 a.m. on 30 December 1896, provides an example of how one death can have a profound political and social impact on an entire nation. Rizal's death by firing squad at Bagumbayan Field was soon transformed into an act of martyrdom, becoming a founding story for the fledgling semi-independent state of the Philippines. He was subsequently described on a photograph as 'the Philippine Joan of Arc'. The black-and-white photo, supposedly of the moment before his actual execution, has taken on iconic, even sacred, status (Figure 14). Through his death Rizal became a national hero for the evolving 'imagined community' of the Philippines.

There are a number of reasons why this talented multilingual 35-year-old (1861–96) was executed. He was a passionate advocate for reform in the Philippines during Spanish colonial rule. He wrote many essays, poems, and letters, but is best known for his two novels, *Noli Me Tangere* (1887) and its sequel *El Filibusterismo* (1891, also known as *The Reign of Greed*). After reading

14. Photo depicting the execution of José Rizal on 30 December 1896, in Manila, at Bagombayan (later called Luneta, then renamed again in his honour as Rizal Park)

Harriet Beecher Stowe's anti-slavery tale *Uncle Tom's Cabin* (1852), Rizal decided to write novels as a way of challenging the status quo within the Philippines. His books were deeply controversial because they highlighted the injustices of Spanish rule and the church's role in helping to subjugate the populace. Banned in the Philippines, they were published in Europe and smuggled into the country. Rizal was arrested on his return from exile in 1896, in the midst of what was turning into an armed revolution, and was convicted of 'rebellion, sedition and conspiracy', even though his support of a violent Philippine uprising was ambivalent.

The afterlife of Rizal's death is a prime example of how martyrdoms are created and politicized, and continually evolve. His martyrdom became a form of political resistance in the colonial world. Some used his death for political ends, others for religious purposes. Since his execution, stories about Rizal have been regularly recited, amplified, and elaborated both in and outside the Philippines. Such stories invariably take on a life of their own, reappearing in unexpected places. Rizal's martyrdom was retold in many different forms, and continues to be expressed through a range of materials.

Statues and other monuments were built; a plaque marking the place where he actually fell was commissioned; and banknotes, coins, postcards, and stamps were produced featuring his face or figure. Just as it is now possible to buy mementoes of recent local martyrs on the West Bank, so in modern-day Manila you can purchase posters, T-shirts, and mugs emblazoned with Rizal's face. These material amplifications rarely remain static and are regularly renewed to speak to subsequent generations of Filipinos. Such revivifications reinvigorate and preserve the memory of Rizal's life and death.

The stories associated with Rizal were also elaborated upon in several films (e.g., *Jose Rizal*, 1998, directed by Marilou Diaz-Abaya) and in works of art. For example, the national artist known as 'Botong', Carlos V. Francisco (1912–69), portrayed the moment of Rizal's execution (Figure 15). The neatly dressed figure of Rizal dominates the picture; his executioners are in the background. As his hat tumbles off his head, the look on his face is a mixture of pain and self-control. The figure of Rizal himself is thrown forward and upwards, almost inviting viewers to lean forward to catch him before he crumples to the ground.

This picture is displayed at a modern museum built at Fort Santiago in Manila, created to house some of the memorabilia

**15. Carlos 'Botong' Francisco, *The Martyrdom of Rizal*, painting. Santiago Fort**

from Rizal's life and death. As part of the centennial celebration of Rizal's martyrdom and the Philippine Revolution, the shrine-like museum was renovated in 1996. Apart from the replica cell, there are numerous objects preserved in glass cases, such as an original copy of *Noli*, sculptures by Rizal, and perhaps more poignantly a 'secular relic', a bone of Rizal's with a bullet wound enshrined in a glass urn. It is possible literally to follow in Rizal's footsteps from his small prison cell in Fort Santiago. There are brass footprints inlaid in the road leading out from the fort of his final incarceration towards the place where he was shot. Both pilgrims and tourists follow this route, walking through the old walled city, *intramuros*, passing many crammed minibuses and horse-drawn carriages touting for tourists, to the actual spot of his execution. Thousands pay different kinds of visual homage to the museum, to the place of execution, and to the nearby monument (which contains his remains) in Rizal Park in Manila.

The monument has been the venue for many eulogies elaborating Rizal's life and death. For instance, Camilos Osias, a local dignitary, gave an address entitled 'Rizal, Martyr to Human Liberty' on 27 April 1953, asserting that:

> Rizal was a martyr in fact and in truth. In infancy, in youth, and in manhood he witnessed the martyrdom of his people and bitter anguish was brought home to his family. He himself was the victim. He was ridiculed and maligned. He was persecuted and exiled. He was imprisoned and tried on trumped up charges. He was tortured, sentenced to death, and done to death. His influence continues. His spirit is immortal. Rizal was not born to die... Rizal, the patriot, the hero, the martyr lives. He will never die.

The allusions to a 1st-century storyteller who was himself persecuted and executed in occupied Palestine are hard to miss, and illustrate how Rizal's martyrdom was often paralleled with Jesus' death. Part of the attraction of Rizal's death is the fact that he is perceived as an innocent martyr in a country steeped in

Catholic piety. His memory lives on. The story of an innocent executed by an oppressive regime has a long pedigree in the Philippines. Several different Filipino groups (so-called *Rizalistas*) went even further in their devotion to Rizal, weaving complex theological narratives around his life and death.

The story of Rizal's execution reverberated particularly powerfully following the assassination of Benigno Aquino on 21 August 1983, just a few minutes after he arrived at Manila International Airport. As with Rizal, public spaces were transformed or changed to mark his death. The airport was later renamed Ninony Aquino International Airport in his honour. Returning from his three-year exile in the USA, he admitted to the accompanying journalists on the plane: 'My feeling is we all have to die sometime and if it's my fate to die by an assassin's bullet, so be it.' Aquino personally linked his own story with that of Rizal, who had likewise returned home from exile to face death. Following his assassination, many other commentators made the same connection. It was later pointed out that just as Rizal's death marked the beginning of the end for Spanish rule, so Aquino's death marked the beginning of the end of Ferdinand Marcos' (1917–89) twenty-year autocratic rule over his own people. These parallel narratives are told and woven together in many places.

The fact that Rizal's death was almost immediately framed as a martyrdom with political, religious, and cultural significance makes it a valuable example for those reflecting on how martyrs are created and politicized. Stories about martyrdoms do not remain still and are never owned by only one individual or group. They are amplified in many different forms for numerous ends. Some even claim that his martyrdom was publicized by the Americans (who briefly replaced the Spanish as colonial rulers of the Philippines) above other local martyrdoms as he represented a non-violent model for leadership in a nation divided by violent revolution. The stories about Rizal have also been creatively elaborated upon, becoming sites of devotion, celebration, commemoration, persuasion, and contest. Knowing some of the many ways in which Rizal's martyrdom is repeated and amplified elaborated sheds light on how other martyrdom stories work.

It is clear from each of the examples in this chapter that the apparent ending of a life can mark the beginning of a new earthly afterlife. In the words of the former Indian prime minister Indira Gandhi (1917–84), herself killed by two of her own bodyguards: 'Martyrdom does not end something, it is only a beginning.' The more writers, speakers, and artists that reimagine a martyr's last days or hours, and circulate details of their death and final words, the brighter the memory shines. Different communities preserve, pass on, and invest social capital into particular deaths, increasing their worth. Once a death is described as a martyrdom, value and significance are added to the martyr's life. Such stories are commonly used to bolster or to subvert the status quo. In other words, behind a claim about the religious significance of a particular martyrdom lies the desire either to reinforce or to challenge the political powers that control a community or nation. Some would even argue that all martyrdoms are political, or at least can be politicized. Martyrs do indeed have the potential to rule from their graves, but they require support from the living to do so.

# Chapter 7
# Questioning martyrdom

Any account of martyrdom will inevitably be selective. Numerous well-known examples and countless lesser-known instances will be left out. A comprehensive history of martyrdom found across different religious traditions, political settings, and cultural contexts would need to be a multi-volume work. The boundaries of who to include and who to exclude would be open to question. This is a commonly debated topic. Two examples stand out. First, should the six million Jews killed during the Second World War *Shoah*, or Holocaust, be described as martyrs or heroes or both? The full English title of the Yad Vashem memorial in Jerusalem brings these titles together: 'The Holocaust Martyrs' and Heroes' Remembrance Authority'. Secondly, should the hundreds of thousands of Tutsi and moderate Hutu killed during the 100-day genocide in Rwanda in April 1994 be remembered as martyrs? Thousands were killed in churches, where they had sought sanctuary. While some priests and nuns were involved in perpetrating the genocide, many of those killed in early April were religious leaders who had acted as outspoken critics of the Hutu power movement. How one answers the question 'Who is a martyr?' in both of these examples can reveal how one understands the meaning of martyrdom.

For some, a martyr and a martyrdom are objective empirical realities that can be studied as isolated phenomena; for others martyrdoms and martyrs are largely created by later communities. From both perspectives there can be many different kinds of martyrdom. Who makes a martyr and their martyrdom is a more complicated question than first appears. A number of the individuals discussed in this book embraced death in such a way as to lay the foundation for their end to be described as a martyrdom and for themselves to be thought of as martyrs. Some actively pursued martyrdom while others, when they realized death was inevitable, became more considered in their actions, writing, or speech. Both Charles I and José Rizal may have lost control of their lives, but they attempted to control the way their deaths would be remembered. Others did not have the luxury or time to be able to try to influence their earthly afterlives. The way in which later communities describe and then interpret a death influence whether it is remembered as a martyrdom.

## Touching and preserving martyrdom

Martyrdom touches the victim, the perpetrator, and the spectator in different ways. While we have prison diaries, smuggled notes, and last words from the scaffold, there are, for obvious reasons, no complete first-hand accounts of a martyrdom written by the martyrs themselves. The martyr's viewpoint is inevitably incomplete. Informed by eyewitness accounts, news reports, or pictures, we can only imagine what it might have felt like. For the victim the touch of martyrdom can be light and swift or long and agonizing. For the audience to watch, view, or hear about a martyrdom can be emotionally touching, even unsettling. The killer or executioner may have to face and touch the victim themselves. The tactile memory can remain, even after their performance at what the French philosopher Michel Foucault (1926–84) described as 'the theatre of death' is over. Like many other executioners, Charles's in London wore masks to preserve their anonymity, fearing for their lives from Royalist supporters, while Joan of Arc's executioner in Rouen confessed after her burning in 1431 that he feared for his soul.

Precisely what happens after death for the martyr is a point of speculation for those left behind. Some claim paradise, rebirth, or even further tribulation, others an extinction of consciousness. There is no way of proving beyond doubt what happens to somebody described as a 'martyr' after their death, though the ending of their earthly lives leaves questions for those left to mourn, to criticize, or to wonder. What are left behind are memories, impressions, and physical remains.

How are these preserved? In the Middle Ages, in particular, a martyr's remains were if possible preserved, treasured, and often transformed into objects of devotion. For example, following his murder by four of King Henry II's (1133–89) knights in Canterbury Cathedral on 29 December 1170, Thomas Becket's (c.1118–70) remains were buried at the eastern end of the cathedral's crypt. Concerned that his body might be stolen, the monks ensured that the burial was carried out swiftly, with a stone placed over his tomb. At least one hole was cut through the stone so that pilgrims would be able to kiss the place where Becket was buried.

Becket was canonized in 1173 by Pope Alexander III (c.1100–81), just three years after his murder. Thousands of pilgrims were soon visiting the shrine of the former archbishop of Canterbury. Here was a northern European Norman saint whose remains were a magnet for visitors. The significant increase in the number of visiting pilgrims substantially augmented the wealth of the cathedral and the city of Canterbury. In his lifetime Becket's manner as archbishop had won him few friends, but in death he was venerated as a saint and a martyr. Many held that he could now pray for the living, so becoming a focal point for generous giving. Pilgrims, for example, were able to purchase Becket badges or tokens marking their pilgrimage. By 1220, his bones were transferred into a jewelled golden shrine on a raised platform in the cathedral's specially constructed Trinity Chapel, where offerings also increased. All over Europe cathedrals, abbeys, and other churches found that displaying and selling the relics of martyrs and saints not only attracted pilgrims, but could also be economically beneficial.

## Disseminating and spreading martyrdom

How are stories about martyrdom spread? As we have seen, martyr narratives can circulate through many different kinds of media. While his body was kept at Canterbury, fragments of Thomas Becket's bloodstained clothes, material used to mop up his blood, and even bone material were turned into portable and easily marketable relics. Over the next century over forty ornate containers, called caskets or reliquary chasses, were created to house some of these kinds of relics. Many were made in Limoges, France in the late 12th and early 13th centuries. The earliest and largest of these Becket reliquaries to survive (c.1180) can be seen at the Victoria and Albert Museum (V&A) in London (Figure 16). Scenes of Becket's assassination, burial, and ascent to heaven adorn the outside of this small ornate blue and gold house-shaped reliquary. These scenes were widely copied on later versions, though the number of knights sometimes varies and on at least one of these versions Becket ascends to heaven flanked not by angels but by two pelicans, symbols of the Eucharist, sacrificial death, and even the Resurrection because they bring life to their young with their own blood.

Each casket had its own story. One, for example, was made for Prior Benedict, a witness to Becket's assassination, to take relics with him when he became the abbot of Peterborough Abbey. It was a common wish to be close to relics, which were seen as holy, precious, and spiritually powerful. The man may have departed, but his body remained. Material matters. Few people actually witnessed the killing of Thomas Becket but many wished to see or to touch the physical remains of this celebrity martyr. For those who could not touch his shrine or go on pilgrimage to

16. The Becket Casket, gilt copper and champlevé enamel over wooden core. Limoges, France, c.1180–1190

Canterbury, reminders of his martyrdom could travel in these portable caskets.

In this way both relics and images of Becket travelled swiftly in the first few decades after his death. It was not long before stained glass, wall paintings, and manuscripts were being illustrated with scenes of his life and martyrdom. The V&A's director in London, Alan Borg, claims that there was 'a sort of Becket mania' that 'spread across Europe'. Evidence suggests that within a few decades of his death, the spread of Becket's martyr cult stretched from Iceland and Scotland to Palestine and Italy. Margaret, the queen consort of Sicily (1128–83) was, according to Borg, 'given a miniature Becket reliquary to wear around her neck', while 'many churches were dedicated to him, and a military order of knights was founded in his name'. Becket's memory touched many people's lives, though by the time the humanist Erasmus (c.1466–1536) visited the Becket shrine at Canterbury in the early 16th century he was bemused at the wealth on display and showmanship of one of his guides who introduced him to the relics.

## Deconstructing and categorizing martyrdom

How is martyrdom both deconstructed and categorized? Shrines commemorating martyrdoms, martyrs, and other saints can become sites of 'idolatry' to be shattered and treasure troves to be plundered. The story that Becket or at least his bones were summoned to face Henry VIII for crimes against the king is probably apocryphal. It is more certain that in September 1538, during the dissolution of the monasteries, Becket's shrine was demolished and his bones moved from where they had rested for over 300 years by Henry VIII's royal commissioners for the destruction of shrines. Controversy remains over whether some of Becket's bones survived, having been smuggled to safety and hidden elsewhere. Deconstructing martyrdom was financially expedient for Henry VIII. His commissioners appear to have used over twenty carts to remove all the gold, silver, and other valuables that had been left at Becket's shrine, particularly by those thankful to this saint for their healing. The deconstruction of martyrdom did not stop with Henry VIII. Deconstruction takes different forms. Attempts may be made to prevent the establishment of martyr cults by completely disposing of the body, as can be seen by the burial of Osama bin Laden (1957–2011) at sea. This did not change the fact that within a few days some groups were celebrating him as a *shaheed* (martyr) and claiming that his death was a martyrdom. Others attempt to disrupt the cult around a martyr by tarnishing the person's reputation, as can be seen in several post-Reformation texts highlighting 'pseudo-martyrs' (see Chapter 5).

As martyr relics became endangered in parts of early modern Europe, their preservation, protection, and categorization became more urgent. Some were described technically as 'first-class relics', which include the bone fragments of saints and martyrs, and relics associated with the life of Christ. For example, the body parts of several English Catholic martyrs from the 16th century are still preserved in Lancashire and Yorkshire. There is sometimes controversy as to who owns the 'original'. For instance, there is debate over whether the mummified hand at Ladyewell, near Preston, or that at the Bar Convent, York, is Margaret Clitherow's right hand, preserved after her execution in 1586. A 'second-class relic' might be an item owned or worn by a martyr, such as the gloves of the Charles I. (Third-class relics are anything that touches first or second class relics). There are debates as to whether such categorizations can be applied to secular martyrs such as José Rizal (see Chapter 6), whose bone fragment with an embedded bullet is preserved in a museum reliquary.

There are other ways of categorizing martyrdom. Through this book we have encountered a wide range of martyrdoms: founding or proto-martyrdoms, legendary or hagiographical martyrdoms, spiritual and military martyrdoms, predatory and pseudo-martyrdoms, as well as new secular and political martyrdoms. This is by no means a comprehensive list or a watertight set of categorizations. We have seen how these categories can be deconstructed and how the precise meaning of the word 'martyrdom' has evolved within several religious traditions, accentuating the debates and controversies surrounding martyrdom.

## Adapting and translating martyrdom

How are stories about martyrdom adapted and translated? Becket's bones may have disappeared but his memory was not only preserved and disseminated: it has also been adapted and translated. Edward Grim, a clerk visiting from Cambridge, provides the only written eyewitness account in his *Life of Thomas Becket, Archbishop of Canterbury and Martyr*, translated from the Latin, *Vita S. Thomae, Cantuariensis Archepiscopi et Martyris*.

Grim portrays Becket's death as both voluntary and noble. Becket refused to have the doors closed or to allow the cathedral to be turned into a 'fortress'. Grim describes how 'the martyr displayed the virtue of perseverance' and offered his body to the killers, 'because he abandoned the world', and 'the world, wanting to overpower him, unknowingly elevated him'. Here is a claim that resonates with an earlier discussion considering whether martyrs can rule after their deaths.

Stories about martyrdom are constantly being adapted and translated into new and sometimes absorbing communicative forms. They often act more as a mirror of the time in which they were produced than as a historical record of the time that they purport to represent. The 1964 film *Becket* (directed by Peter Glenville), based on the French 1959 play *Becket or the Honor of God* (by Jean Anouilh) may not follow Grim's account but Richard Burton's portrayal of the archbishop as he dies at the hands of the knights is full of dignified pathos. It reflects a world divided between church and state, where a 'cold war' swiftly becomes overheated.

Unlike the 1964 film, T. S. Eliot's 1935 play *Murder in the Cathedral* draws more detail from Grim's account. It reflects one man bravely facing up to an authoritarian regime, resonating with the political situation in Europe during the 1930s. One recorded version includes a powerful performance by the actor Robert Donat, who played Becket in the 1953 stage version at the Old Vic in London. Donat struggled with chronic asthma, which enriched the pathos in his voice, especially when Becket preaches on Christmas Day about halfway through the play. He speaks about the joy ('rejoicing') and sorrow ('mourning') of martyrdom and claims that martyrdom can never be accidental, subtly predicting his own death. Earlier in the play Becket has already rejected four tempters who offer him physical safety, power, riches, and, intriguingly, glory through martyrdom. This is the greatest temptation for Becket: 'To do the right deed for the wrong reason.' Both the stage and film rendition of Becket's story elaborated on his story and his death.

## Spiritualizing and militarizing martyrdom

Why martyrdom often brings together devotion and violence can be seen in several contrasting examples. When Joan of Arc (c.1412–31), 'the Maid of Orléans', was burnt at the stake in Rouen at the age of 19, the authorities wished to ensure that no cult would arise around her remains. So they burnt her body several times over and then threw her ashes, and some claim her heart, into the river Seine. Even though there was nothing left of Joan to touch, this was not enough to erase her memory. A retrial in 1456 ensured that she was declared innocent and a martyr. The extensive written records of her trial, execution, and retrial have been preserved and have contributed to the cult that has surrounded her memory.

Her death has been put to many different uses over the last four centuries, both spiritual and military. As a saint Joan is prayed to and, as a soldier who inspired the lifting of the Siege of Orléans in 1429, she is often admired. Not only in France but also in other parts of the world the figure of Joan as a military martyr has been recycled at times of national emergency. Her portrait, however, is constantly being reconfigured to suit local needs and expectations. Over thirty-five films have been made about her life and martyrdom. For example, Cecil B. DeMille's film *Joan the Woman* (1916) was significantly adapted between its release in the USA and its distribution in France. The French version simplified the plot and celebrated Joan as a self-sacrificing and maternal national heroine, to appeal to a people engaged in a war for national survival. Her figure would again change in George Bernard Shaw's play *Saint Joan*, Carl Theodor Dreyer's silent film of *The Passion of Joan of Arc* (1928) (Figure 17), then Robert Bresson's *The Trial of Joan of Arc* (1962), and more recently Luc Besson's *The Messenger: The Story of Joan of Arc* (1999).

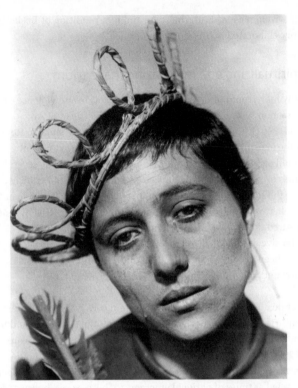

**17. Maria Falconetti in *La Passion de Jeanne d'Arc* (*The Passion of Joan of Arc*), 1928**

In the same year as DeMille's *Joan* film appeared in war-torn Europe one of the less well-known English First World War poets Robert Nichols wrote 'The Last Salute' while serving at Ypres, bringing together both spiritual and military views of martyrdom. He claims that even though he may die anonymous and alone 'the soldier is the Martyr of a nation'. The martyr who picks up the sword in one hand and the metaphorical cross in the other resonates with accounts and sermons from the Middle Ages where it was not uncommon for crusading knights who lost their lives to be designated as 'martyrs'. Some believed that they were following in the footsteps of the military martyrs and patrons of the crusades St George of Lydda and St Demetrius of Thessaloniki. Even the executed leaders of the 1916 Irish Easter Rising in Dublin are also widely described in Ireland as 'martyrs', celebrated as both military and spiritual freedom fighters.

This combining of spiritual and military descriptions of martyrdom is not restricted to Europe and stretches to primarily politically motivated groups. Consider the so-called 'Fathers of Suicide Bomb Attacks', the Liberation Tamil Tigers of Eelam (LTTE), who have been behind over 240 suicide attacks. The Tamil Tigers were largely politically motivated, fighting for an independent state free from the Sinhalese in the north of Sri Lanka. Those who died in the struggle were described as 'martyrs', planted like 'seeds' to bring life and independence to the motherland. The late leader of the LTTE, Thiruvenkadam Veluppillai Prabhakaran (1954–2009), declared on Remembrance Day in 1992 that those who have sown the seeds for the rise of a very great liberation 'should be worshipped in the temples of our hearts throughout the ages'.

Devotion towards military martyrs who kill others is a practice that is open to question within most, if not all, religious traditions. For some the spiritualizing of military, aggressive, or predatory approaches to martyrdom is a comparatively recent phenomenon. From this point of view the 'pure form' of non-violent martyrdom has been corrupted. For others the ambiguities of spiritualizing a military martyr is not such a new occurrence. Along with the examples of Joan of Arc and the Tamil Tigers, the actions of Samson, the Masada rebels, the combat arena gladiators, zealous violent monks, crusading martyrs, and the Karbala fighters are all used as evidence to support the hypothesis that the tension between violent and non-violent understandings of martyrdom has a long history within each of the Abrahamic traditions. Nevertheless, the non-violent approach embodied by many different martyrs does interrogate the military uses of martyrdom.

## Suffering and healing martyrdoms

How is suffering represented and changed through martyrdom? It is striking how some accounts of martyrdom represent the martyr either as not suffering or as enduring suffering with great composure. Jewish accounts from the Middle Ages describe how some Jewish martyrs would not burn, reminding readers of the three young men who survived the fiery furnace in the book of Daniel. According to one early Christian account, Laurence (225–58), one of seven deacons martyred under Emperor Valerian in 258, was roasted on a gridiron. He even joked, 'turn me over ... I'm done on this side'. Even if this description is based on a scribal error, as many scholars now believe, that this statement has often been repeated reveals a recurring attitude towards suffering and pain. As in many other early Christian accounts of martyrdom, the martyr remains steadfast and even more noble in the midst of suffering. By contrast, the accounts of Christians martyring Christians in the post-Reformation era (see Chapter 5) are examples of a narrator depicting the agony in more revealing detail. Nevertheless, a number of 16th- and 17th-century portrayals of martyrs showed them not in pain but either sitting peacefully close to their instruments of torture (e.g., Caravaggio's St Catherine next to her wheel: see Fig. 9) or wounded, cared for, and almost dying (e.g., in George de La Tour's *St Sebastian Tended by St Irene*, *c*.1649; Figure 18). Such imagery raises questions as to how communities should respond to violence and persecution today. These are also useful reminders that the way suffering is understood and represented has a complex history.

Contemporary Western approaches to suffering can be questioned when confronted by unexpected calmness when facing extreme pain. Consider, for example, the self-immolation of the 73-year-old Buddhist monk Thích Quảng Đức on a busy street in Saigon (now Ho Chi Minh City), Vietnam, in 1963. He was protesting against the harsh treatment of Buddhist monks by

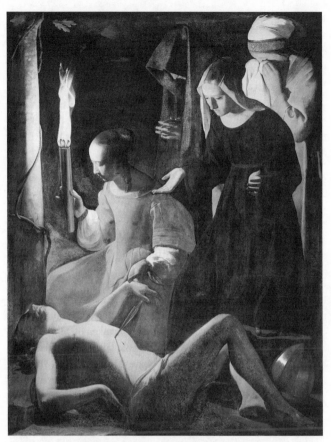

18. Georges de la Tour, *St Sebastian Tended by St Irene*, oil on canvas *c.*1649. This picture goes beyond the common practice of depicting Sebastian pierced by several arrows and still tied to a post or a tree. According to the fifth-century *Acts of Sebastian* (widely agreed to be legendary), the arrows did not kill him and Irene tended Sebastian back to health; though on the orders of the emperor Diocletian, he was then bludgeoned to death and his body disposed of down a sewer (*c.*288). Only many centuries later would he become the martyr saint turned to for protection from the plague

**19. Thích Quảng Đức during his self-immolation, on a street in Saigon, Vietnam, (now Ho Chi Minh City), 11 June 1963**

the Roman Catholic-dominated Vietnamese government. A black-and-white photograph, which captured him remaining absolutely still in the midst of the flame, became internationally famous through a Pulitzer Prize-winning photograph taken by Malcolm Browne (b.1933) (Figure 19). A similar photo taken seconds later by Browne, when the flames had taken hold of Quảng Đức body, also won him the 1963 World Press Photo Award. The image raises several different questions: Is this is a public suicide or a self-inflicted martyrdom leading to enlightenment? And, more practically, how is it possible to endure such heat and pain without writhing in agony?

Representations of martyrdom in Sikhism also commonly represent the martyr enduring their execution in complete control of their bodies and emotions. The fifth Guru, Arjan Dev (1563–1606), normally described as the first Sikh martyr, stands out in this respect. The Mogul emperor of India Jahangir ordered that the Guru be both tortured and executed for refusing to remove all Hindu and Islamic references from their 'holy book'. While there are debates about how he died, he is commonly represented as simply

**20. Gurvinder Pal Singh, *Torture of Guru Arjan Dev*, painting, no date.**
This picture depicts the Guru sitting on a red hot sheet of iron with
scalding sand being poured over his body. It is believed that this
torture took place in the prison of Lahore under the Mogul emperor of
India Jahangir. The Guru's calm poise in the face of torture is
commonly represented artistically. From the Central Sikh Museum,
Amritsar

sitting on a hot sheet or in a cauldron above a fire and looking out
with compassion towards the viewer (Figure 20). Guru Arjan Dev is
believed also to have had boiling hot sand or water poured over his
body. It is claimed that he endured this torture for five days until he
was finally taken for a wash in the river, only to disappear never to
be seen again. Many Sikhs now claim that through his martyrdom
he 'gave birth to thousands of martyrs in the Sikh faith'. Every
year his story is commemorated by Sikhs who offer drinks to
passers-by in the heat of the day. It is also used to celebrate a
martyr who gave his life for interreligious understanding in India
and beyond. His death, as described by later generations also
interrogated the use of state force against a weaker body.

Like Guru Arjan Dev's story, other memories of martyrs are
sometimes invoked in an attempt both to question and to heal

divided nations. For instance, a few days before his murder by a marksman in the hospital chapel while celebrating the late afternoon Mass on 24 March 1980, the Salvadorian archbishop Oscar Romero (1917–80) was interviewed by a journalist for the Mexican newspaper *Excelsior*. He admitted he had often been threatened with death, though

> I do not believe in death without resurrection. If I am killed, I shall arise in the Salvadoran people...Martyrdom is a grace of God that I do not believe that I deserve. But if God accepts the sacrifice of my life, let my blood be the seed of freedom and the sign that hope will still be a reality.

While some claimed that he contributed to the healing of the nation, other religious and political leaders in El Salvador refused to acknowledge him as a martyr.

21. Statues of modern martyrs above the Great West Door, Westminster Abbey. From left to right: Archbishop Janani Luwum of Uganda, Grand Duchess Elizabeth of Russia, Dr Martin Luther King Jr, Archbishop Óscar Romero, Dietrich Bonhoeffer, Esther John of Pakistan, and Lucian Tapiedi of Papua New Guinea. London, 1998

Nevertheless, his reputation rapidly spread around the world, as can be seen above the Great West Door of Westminster Abbey in London: one of the ten 20th-century martyr statues is of Romero (Figure 21). Created in 1998, it stands between statues of the African American Rights campaigner Martin Luther King, Jr, assassinated in Memphis, Tennessee, and the German theologian Dietrich Bonhoeffer, executed in a concentration camp only a few weeks before the end of the Second World War. Romero's life, his statements, and his voice, like so many others discussed in this book, are remembered far more because of the way he died than in themselves. His comments eight months before his murder might have been forgotten if he had lived, but instead they continue to circle the globe: 'It is very easy to kill, especially when one has weapons, but how hard it is to let oneself be killed for love of the people.'

# Further reading

## Chapter 1: Debating martyrdom and Chapter 2: Portraying martyrdom

Sara Ahbel-Rappe and Rachana Kamtekar (eds.), *A Companion to Socrates* (Oxford: Blackwell, 2006). Useful set of essays, including discussion of 'The Trial and Death of Socrates' (by Debra Nails) and 'Picturing Socrates' (by Kenneth Lapatin).

Daniel Boyarin, *Dying for God: Martyrdom and the Making of Christianity and Judaism* (Stanford: Stanford University Press, 1999). Boyarin argues that a discourse of martyrology in the 1st century resulted in cultural and religious developments within and between the Jewish and Christian communities, enabling them both to establish a unique self-definition.

Jeremy Cohen, *Sanctifying the Name of God: Jewish Martyrs and Jewish Memories of the First Crusade* (Philadelphia: University of Pennsylvania Press, 2004).

Arthur J. Droge and James D. Tabor, *A Noble Death: Suicide and Martyrdom among Christian and Jews in Antiquity* (San Francisco: HarperCollins, 1992). This book explores the idea of suicide in antiquity, exploring when and whether it was 'noble'. The authors explore the relations between contemporary attitudes towards voluntary death to those found in the Judaeo-Christian tradition as represented in the Bible.

Susan Einbinder, *Beautiful Death: Jewish Poetry and Martyrdom in Medieval France* (Princeton: Princeton University Press, 2002). Einbinder explores how many within Jewish communities in the Rhine Valley chose suicide rather than murder at the hands of the crusading mobs. This book analyses the poetic and literary commemoration of these medieval Jewish martyrs.

Jan Willem van Henten, *The Maccabean Martyrs as the Saviours of the Jewish People: A Study of 2 and 4 Maccabees* (Leiden: Brill, 1997). This book examines the religious, political, and philosophical aspects of noble death as found in 2 and 4 Maccabees with reference to non-Jewish traditions.

Jan Willem van Henten and Friedrich Avemarie, *Martyrdom and Noble Death: Selected Texts from Graeco-Roman, Jewish, and Christian Antiquity* (London: Routledge, 2002). This book explores the phenomenon of noble death in pagan, Jewish, and Christian sources. It covers a wide chronological range and its cross-cultural approach provides a useful collection of texts in one volume.

Plato, *The Last Days of Socrates* (London: Penguin, 2003). Plato's account of Socrates' trial and death in 399 BCE through four dialogues, including the *Apology* and *Phaedo*.

Shmuel Shepkaru, *Jewish Martyrs in the Pagan and Christian Worlds* (Cambridge: Cambridge University Press, 2006). Through a linear and careful history of Jewish martyrdom from the Hellenistic period to the High Middle Ages, Shepkaru critically analyses the claim that martyrdom originated in the Hellenistic Jewish world.

Lacey Baldwin Smith, *Fools, Martyrs, Traitors: The Story of Martyrdom in the Western World* (Evanston, IL: Northwestern University Press, 2009). Smith analyses the political motivations, personalities, and psychology of martyrs, in an attempt to understand the willingness to die to sanctify a deity, defend a cause, or prove a point.

## Chapter 3: Remembering martyrdom

Timothy D. Barnes, *Early Christian Hagiography and Roman History* (Tübingen: Mohr Siebeck, 2010). This book provides a detailed and critical study of early ancient sources for the history of Christianity, including several Martyrdom stories, in the Roman Empire.

Glen W. Bowersock, *Martyrdom and Rome* (Cambridge: Cambridge University Press, 1995). This book examines the historical context of the early Christian martyrs in relation to everyday life and beliefs in the Roman Empire. Bowerstock also compares the Graeco-Roman background with the martyrologies of both Jews and Muslims. He argues that martyrdom emerged not out of Judaism but rather out of 2nd-century Christianity within the Graeco-Roman world, especially in Asia Minor.

Michael L. Budde and Karen Scott (eds), *Witness of the Body: The Past, Present and Future of Christian Martyrdom* (Grand Rapids, MI: Eerdmans, 2011). This is a collection of essays exploring the relation between martyrdom and the church.

Elizabeth Castelli, *Martyrdom and Memory: Early Christian Culture Making* (New York: Columbia University Press, 2004). This book explores how the collective memories of martyrdom and persecution contributed to the development of Christian ideas, institutions, and cultural forms. Castelli shows how the making of martyrdoms challenged the Roman Empire. She also draws on more recent killings to analyse how the martyr can be placed at the centre of religion.

William H. C. Frend, *Martyrdom and Persecution in the Early Church* (Oxford: Blackwell, 1965). This book explores why so many early Christians not only accepted but actually welcomed martyrdom. Frend examines the Jewish roots of Christian martyrdom and discusses a number of major persecutions in the second, third, and fourth centuries. He argues that 'Judaism was itself a religion of martyrdom', and therefore the 'Jewish psychology of martyrdom' was a vital foundation for Christian martyrdom. (This study is commonly contrasted with Bowersock's approach.)

Michael Gaddi, *'There is No Crime for Those who have Christ': Religious Violence in the Christian Roman Empire* (Berkeley and Los Angeles: University of California Press, 2005). Gaddi provides an analysis of religious violence and the beliefs behind it to be found in the Christian Roman Empire of the fourth and fifth centuries, including a discussion of martyrdom and persecution prior to and leading up to this period. He shows how the asceticism of martyrdom could also lead to acts of violence.

Lucy Grig, *Making Martyrs in Late Antiquity* (London: Duckworth, 2004). Grig argues that the period of the post-Constantinian fourth and early fifth centuries can be referred to as 'the era of the martyrs' by examining sources from the Latin West such as sermons, hagiographical texts, visual representations, and poetry.

Doron Mendels, *The Media Revolution of Early Christianity: An Essay on Eusebius' Ecclesiastical History* (Grand Rapids, MI: Eerdmans, 1999).

Paul Middleton, *Radical Martyrdom and Cosmic Conflict in Early Christianity* (T. & T. Clark: London, 2006). Middleton discusses the different views of radical martyrdom in the early church, partly by re-examining Christian martyrdom within the heritage of Jewish War tradition.

Candida R. Moss, *Ancient Christian Martyrdom: Diverse Practices, Theologies and Traditions* (New Haven: Yale University Press, 2012). Moss examines the diverse perspectives of what it meant to die for Christ during the first and second centuries. Several scholarly narratives about the spread of martyrdom are called into question by exploring the distinctive and diverging theologies of martyrdom in different congregations.

Alison Trites, *The New Testament Concept of Witness* (Cambridge: Cambridge University Press, 2004). In this book Trites traces the different ways in which 'witness' and 'testimony' are used within the New Testament. She examines these terms in relation to ancient legal practice, and considers, for example, how far 'witness' or 'martyr' should be understood in the light of texts within the Hebrew bible.

## Chapter 4: Contesting martyrdom

Kamran Scot Aghaie, *The Martyrs of Karbala: Shi'i Symbols and Rituals in Modern Iran* (Seattle: University of Washington Press, 2004). This study reveals how modernization has influenced the societal, political, and religious culture of Iran. It includes a thorough examination of the changes, which have taken place in Shi'i rituals and symbols over the past two centuries.

Madawi Al-Rasheed and Marat Shterin, *Dying for Faith: Religiously Motivated Violence in the Contemporary World* (London: I. B. Tauris, 2009). This collection of essays examines the contexts in which religiously motivated violence is expressed, enacted, and reported. It provides perspectives from Islam to Buddhism to new Western religious movements.

Mia Bloom, *Dying to Kill: the Allure of Suicide Terror* (New York; Columbia University Press, 2005).

Gary Bunt, *Islam in the Digital Age: E-jihad, Online Fatwas, and Cyber Islamic Environments* (London: Pluto Press, 2003). Bunt discusses the multiple uses of the Internet within Islamic cultures, including various online discussions of martyrdom. He considers conflicting understandings of Islamic religious authority and the uses of 'on-line fatwas'. He also analyses different forms of 'e-jihad' (or 'electronic jihad'), which result in online activism, from promoting violence and celebrating martyrdoms to coordinating peaceful Islamic protests and expression.

David Cook, *Martyrdom in Islam* (Cambridge: Cambridge University Press, 2007). Cook's analysis of martyrdom shows how the ideas surrounding it have evolved to suit the historical circumstances. Discussions about the earliest martyrdom traditions, including Jewish and Christian traditions, and definitions of martyrdom precede an analysis of the different world-views of Sunnis and Shi'ites.

David Cook and Olivia Allison, *Understanding and Addressing Suicide Attacks: The Faith and Politics of Martyrdom Operations* (Westport, CT: Praeger, 2007). This work addresses the historical, religious, and political background of suicide attacks. It also offers critiques of the media coverage, policy approaches, and attempts to combat suicide missions.

Farhad Khosrakhavar, *Suicide Bombers: Allah's New Martyrs*, trans. D. Macey (London: Pluto Press, 2005). Interviews with jailed Islamist militants show the different attitudes towards martyrdom in different countries (including Iran, Palestine, Lebanon, and Egypt). It also provides insight into different understandings of martyrdom between martyrs from the developing world and those from the Western world.

Assaf Moghadam, *The Globalization of Martyrdom: Al Qaeda, Salafi Jihad, and the Diffusion of Suicide Attacks* (Baltimore: Johns Hopkins University Press, 2008). This in-depth analysis of the rise and spread of suicide attacks investigates the relationship between ideology and suicide strikes, particularly on a global level.

Robert Pape, *The Strategic Logic of Suicide Terrorism* (New York: Random House, 2005).

Thomas Sizgorich, *Violence and Belief in Late Antiquity: Militant Devotion in Christianity and Islam* (Philadelphia: University of Pennsylvania Press, 2009). Why and how did 'violent expressions of religious devotion' become 'central to the self-understandings of both Christian and Muslim communities between the fourth and ninth centuries'? Sizgorich analyses the 'cultivation of violent martyrdom as a path to holiness' in both Christian and Islamic traditions.

Roxanne Varzi, *Warring Souls: Youth, Media, and Martyrdom in Post-Revolution Iran* (Durham, NC: Duke University Press, 2006). Varzi explores different perspectives in relation to martyrdom in Iran, drawing upon films, documentaries, and posters.

Brian Wicker (ed.), *Witnesses to Faith? Martyrdom in Christianity and Islam* (Aldershot: Ashgate, 2006). Christian and Islamic scholars explore what is meant by martyrdom today. These essays investigate historical and contemporary issues relating to martyrdom for both traditions. One intriguing recurring question is whether martyrs from one tradition would recognize martyrs from the other tradition as such.

## Chapter 5: Reforming martyrdom

Anne Dillon, *The Construction of Martyrdom in the English Catholic Community, 1535–1603* (Aldershot: Ashgate, 2002).

Eamon Duffy, *Fires of Faith: Catholic England under Mary Tudor* (New Haven: Yale University Press, 2009). Duffy offers a fresh perspective on the martyrdoms under the reign of Queen Mary.

John Foxe, *The Unabridged Acts and Monuments Online* (*TAMO*) (Sheffield: HRI Online Publications, 2011) <http//www.johnfoxe.org> accessed 17 May 2011. This valuable resource provides easy access to the full text and illustrations of all four editions of *Foxe's Book of Martyrs*, as well as detailed commentary, critical essays, and further resources.

John Foxe, *Foxe's Book of Martyrs: Select Narratives* (Oxford: Oxford University Press, 2009). This modernized and selective version of Foxe's work also provides a comprehensive introduction to his life.

Brad S. Gregory, *Salvation at Stake: Christian Martyrdom in Early Modern Europe* (Cambridge, MA: Harvard University Press, 1999). This book explores the similarities and differences between Protestant, Catholic, and Anabaptist martyrs.

John N. King, *Foxe's 'Book of Martyrs' and Early Modern Print Culture* (Cambridge: Cambridge University Press, 2006). King investigates 'how the compilation of texts accumulated under Foxe's supervision came, when published, to exert such a powerful influence on the consciousness of Early Modern England'. It also includes detailed discussions of Foxe's text and the illustrations.

Susannah Brietz Monta, *Martyrdom and Literature in Early Modern England* (Cambridge: Cambridge University Press, 2005). Monta analyses how Protestant and Catholic martyrs were represented during and after the Reformation, arguing that Protestant and Catholic texts developed through dialogue and even competition 'across the religious divide'.

Adrian Chastain Weimer, *Martyrs' Mirror: Persecution and Holiness in Early New England* (Oxford: Oxford University Press, 2011). Weimer considers how a range of martyrs' books were read, used, and interpreted in New England.

## Chapter 6: Politicizing martyrdom

Benedict Anderson, *Imagined Communities: Reflections on the Origins and Spread of Nationalism* (London: Verso, 2010).

Susan Dunn, *The Deaths of Louis XVI: Regicide and the French Political Imagination* (Princeton: Princeton University Press, 1994).

Thomas Freeman and Thomas Mayer (eds), *Martyrs and Martyrdom in England, c.1400–1700* (Woodbridge: Boydell Press, 2007). This collection of essays provides analysis of the political, social, and religious backgrounds in England during the period from 1400–1700, exploring how the concept of martyrdom was shaped and used by different religious groups.

Leon Maria Guerrero, *The First Filipino: A Biography of José Rizal* (Manila: National Historical Institute of the Philippines, 1987). This is one of the most authoritative and widely read biographies of José Rizal.

Andrew Lacey, *The Cult of King Charles the Martyr* (Woodbridge: Boydell Press, 2003). A detailed and lucid study that demonstrates how the foundations of the cult of King Charles the martyr were laid before his death and evolved rapidly after his execution.

Robert Massie, *Nicholas and Alexandra* (London: Orion, 1996). Massie provides the story of the last tsar of Russia, with personal family history linked to the collapse of imperial Russia.

David Morgan (ed.), *Key Words in Religion, Media and Culture* (New York and London: Routledge, 2008). This is a useful collection of essays on the relationships between media and religion, including a chapter on 'narrative' in relation to the martyrdom and life of José Rizal.

## Chapter 7: Questioning martyrdom

Michael Biggs, 'Dying without Killing, Self-Immolations 1962–2002', in D. Gambetta (ed.), *Making Sense of Suicide Missions* (Oxford University Press: Oxford, 2005).

Robin Blaetz, *Visions of the Maid: Joan of Arc in American Film and Culture* (Charlottesville: University Press of Virginia, 2001).

Michael P. Jensen, *Martyrdom and Identity* (London: T&T Clark/ Continuum, 2010). Theological reflection structured around T. S. Eliot's play *Murder in the Cathedral*.

Johan Leemans (ed.), *More than a Memory: The Discourse of Martyrdom and the Construction of Christian Identity in the History of Christianity* (Leuven: Peeters, 2005). This volume explores the relationship between the discourse generated by the life of a martyr and the construction of Christian identity. Martyrdom is explored from the 2nd-century martyrdom of Lyons and Vienne to Latin America in the 1960s.

Paul Middleton, *Martyrdom: A Guide for the Perplexed* (London: T&T Clark, 2009). This is a lively and accessible discussion of martyrdom within the Jewish, Christian, and Muslim traditions.

Jolyon Mitchell, *Promoting Peace, Inciting Violence: The Role of Religion and Media* (London and New York: Routledge, 2012). Through a series of international case studies Mitchell analyses how media and religion can combine to incite violence and promote peace. The second chapter includes a detailed discussion of a range of visual representations of martyrdom during the Iran–Iraq War (see also Chapter 4 of this VSI).

Judith Perkins, *The Suffering Self: Pain and Narrative Representation in the Early Christian Era* (London: Routledge, 1995).

Regine Pernoud and Marie-Veronique Clin, *Joan of Arc: Her Story*, trans. J. du Quesnay Adams (Basingstoke: Palgrave Macmillan, 1999). This is an English translation of the best-selling French edition, which includes a glossary of individuals, historical events, and interpretations.

Lena Ross, 'Age before Beauty: A Comparative Study of Martyrs in American Disaster Movies and their Medieval Predecessors', *Journal of Religion and Film*, 11/1 (2007) <http://www.unomaha.edu/jrf/vol11no1/RoosMartyrs.htm> accessed 19 June 2012. Ross argues that Hollywood 'movie martyrs' are significantly different from 'classical Christian martyrs as portrayed in medieval legends'.

Theresa Sanders, *Celluloid Saints: Images of Sanctity in Film* (Macon, GA: Mercer University Press, 2002). Sanders analyses a wide range of films, including several movies portraying martyrs and martyrdoms.

Jon Sobrinoa, *Witnesses to the Kingdom: The Martyrs of El Slavador and the Crucified Peoples* (Maryknoll, NY: Orbis Books, 2003).

Charles Townshend, *Easter 1916: The Irish Rebellion* (London: Allen Lane, 2005). This book traces the events of the Irish Rebellion of 1916 from before the First World War to the aftermath of the War of Independence.

## Some films relating to martyrdom

*Alexander* (2004, Oliver Stone)
*Barefoot in Athens* (1966, George Schaefer)
*Becket* (1964, Peter Glenville)
*Elizabeth* (1998, Shekhar Kapur)
*Four Lions* (2010, Chris Morris)
*Joan of Arc* (1948, Victor Fleming)
*Leily is with me* (1996, Kamal Tabrizi)
*The Making of a Martyr* (2006, Brooke Goldstein and Alistair Leyland)
*The Martyrdom of Nurse Cavell* (1916, John Gavin)
*Martyrs Docu Feature (Shaheed)*, (2012, Sagmeet Singh Samundri)
*The Messenger: The story of Joan of Arc* (1999, Luc Besson)
*Of Gods and Men* (2010, Xavier Beauvois)
*Paradise Now* (2005, Hany Abu-Assad)
*The Passion of Joan of Arc* (1928, Carl Theodor Dreyer)
*Rizal* (1998, Marilou Diaz-Abaya)
*Romero* (1989, John Duigan)
*Saint Joan* (1957, Otto Preminger)
*The Sign of the Cross* (1932, Cecil B. DeMille)
*Socrates* (1970, Robert Rossellini)
*The Trial of Joan of Arc* (1962, Robert Bresson)
*United 93* (2006, Paul Greengrass)

# Index

# Expand your collection of
# VERY SHORT INTRODUCTIONS